SECRET
CONNECTICUT

A Guide to the Weird,
Wonderful, and Obscure

Anastasia Mills Healy

Library of Congress Control Number: 2020950052

ISBN: 9781681063058

Design by Jill Halpin

Printed in the United States of America
21 22 23 24 25 5 4 3 2 1

For my father, who taught me to be curious about the world, and for my children, whom I hope to inspire.

CONTENTS

ACKNOWLEDGMENTS

I'd like to thank all the curators, directors, librarians, and communications officers throughout the state who provided information and photos for this book and reviewed copy.

I'd also like to thank the nonprofits and professional photographers like Kelly Hunt, Deb Key, and ChiChi Ubiña, who waived licensing fees so we could share the enclosed images.

Special shout-outs go to my husband, who tracked down contacts for me; to the total stranger who gave me a tour of his Thimble Island home; and to Martha Moore. A Roebling descendant and president of the board of directors of the Roebling, New Jersey–based Roebling Museum, Moore solved the mystery of the small, pedestrian Brooklyn Bridge in Greenwich.

INTRODUCTION

As a travel writer, I welcomed the opportunity to research and write this book during the coronavirus pandemic. When I couldn't venture safely outside the country, the state, or even my own home, I spent quarantine uncovering intriguing stories about Connecticut's pirates, architecture, history, archaeology, and gastronomy. Taking walks down memory lane, I recalled the joy of Latin Day, the serenity of Enders Island, and eye-opening visits to many of the sights and attractions included here. I've even stayed at Winvian, although not in Helicopter (but I did sit in it!).

I did not know previously about Adriaen Block, Samuel Huntington, Eli Whitney's other invention, or that we fought a war with Pennsylvania for 30 years. Diving horses, Nazi camps on American soil, and a spa resort that John Adams documented also were news to me. The extent of Connecticut's Yankee ingenuity also boggled my mind: We've invented everything from the submarine to the hamburger, the dictionary, and the Wiffle ball. We've started food companies like Pepperidge Farm, Peter Paul, and Subway and businesses that became giants of industry like US Rubber, Timex, and Frontier Communications. I hope readers find these stories as fascinating as I did and come away with a fuller understanding of our great state.

The stories of Martin Luther King Jr.'s summers in Simsbury and of early free Black and Native American communities in Bridgeport, Barkhamsted, and Greenwich are important and should be more widely known. I encountered people working toward that goal: Simsbury High School students who researched and produced a documentary on MLK and inspired a memorial in their town; a community leader championing the preservation of the Mary and Eliza Freeman Houses; the Golden Hill Paugussett Clan Mother; and descendants of residents of the Lighthouse and Hangroot communities. I am grateful to have crossed virtual paths with them and all the others researching P. T. Barnum, F. Scott Fitzgerald, Gustave Whitehead, Theodate Pope, William Gillette, Prudence Crandall, Hiram Bingham, Henry Obookiah, and so many more remarkable and colorful people connected with the state.

Note that at press time, the coronavirus was curtailing the operation of many attractions and establishments discussed in this book. Please check directly with a location before setting out to visit.

UP, UP, AND AWAY

Didn't your last hotel room have a helicopter in it?

Of the 18 themed cottages at Winvian, none is as unique as Helicopter.

Walk in the doorway and, boom, there it is: a real 1968 Sikorsky Sea King Pelican HH3F Coast Guard helicopter.

Climb into the cockpit to see the original controls, switches, and gauges, or step into the back, grab a beverage from the fridge, and kick back on the couch to watch TV.

Unfortunately, no flying is allowed or even possible, as the rotor blades are fixed to the ceiling. But this baby has seen its fair share of action, and Coasties who had actually flown rescue missions on this very helicopter have stayed here as guests.

It's doubtful that the novelty of having a helicopter in your hotel room would wear off, but should you desire other diversions, the 890-square-foot cottage has a screened-in porch, woodburning fireplace, and Jacuzzi tub tucked between the bed and the copter.

Nestled on the property's 113 acres are other cottages, such as Treehouse, perched 35 feet above the forest floor; Maritime, with a bed at the bottom of a lighthouse-like cylinder; and the medieval-themed Connecticut Yankee.

Created by a number of talented architects and designers (Malcolm Appleton was Helicopter's architect), the cabins all are different and come with bicycles for exploring. There's an outdoor pool and spa onsite, a lounge with a pool table

---

J. Newton Williams of Derby built a helicopter that lifted off the ground in 1909; Igor Sikorsky designed and flew the world's first practical helicopter in Stratford in 1939.

One of Winvian's 18 themed cottages has a real Coast Guard helicopter inside, and there's a living area with a TV and bar inside the helicopter. (Top image courtesy of Winvian. Bottom courtesy of Anastasia Mills Healy)

HELLO, HELICOPTER

What: A bar inside a helicopter inside a hotel room

Where: Winvian Farm, 155 Alain White Rd., Morris

Cost: $699–$899 per night

Pro Tip: The nearby White Memorial Foundation is an extraordinary nature preserve.

and board games, and a formal restaurant serving sophisticated international cuisine. Children are welcome during much of the year, but the cabins that easily accommodate them are limited. This rarified, whimsical playground is quite happily inhabited mostly by adults.

A QUARTER ACRE
OF HEARTACHE

Why is there a Native American reservation that's only a quarter of an acre?

Most Connecticans know about the Mohegans and the Mashantucket Pequots, due to their casino complexes in the state, but what about the Golden Hill Paugussetts?

For thousands of years, the tribe lived along the coast in the area that's now Bridgeport, Milford, Stratford, and Fairfield. Oysters, clams, salmon, and shad were bountiful, and the fertile coastal plain produced corn, beans, and squash.

First Dutch traders and then English settlers arrived and relegated the tribe to reservations, beginning in 1639 at Golden Hill (Bridgeport). In 1680, Stratford bisected their 160 acres with Washington Avenue and halved their land. Over the next century, white farmers left the tribe with only eight acres. When a white landowner took up the Paugussetts' cause, he ended up forcing their hand in selling the remainder of their land to pay for his legal representation fees.

In the 1800s, white settlers repeatedly granted and divested the Paugussetts of land. In 1875, after decades of working as a seaman and at other jobs, a Paugussett chief named William Sherman had saved enough money to secure land that contained an ancient burial ground. He built a home on it, and upon his death he deeded it to the state for use in perpetuity as

In 1981, the State of Connecticut granted the Golden Hill Paugussetts 106 acres in Colchester, an hour away.

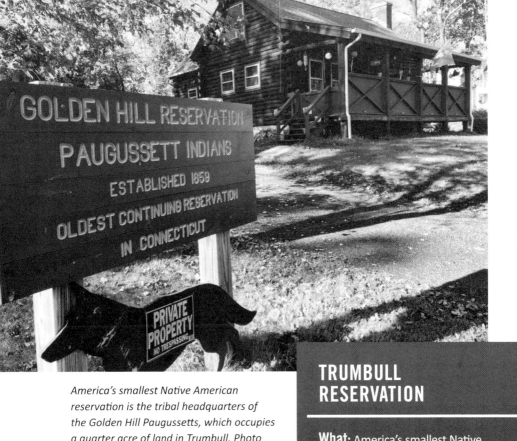

America's smallest Native American reservation is the tribal headquarters of the Golden Hill Paugussetts, which occupies a quarter acre of land in Trumbull. Photo courtesy of Tribal Leader Clan Mother Shoran Waupatuquay Piper.

the Golden Hill Reservation. This quarter of an acre is the home of its chieftain and headquarters of the tribe. In 1985, Claude Clayton Smith authored a history of the tribe, poignantly titled *A Quarter Acre of Heartache*.

The Golden Hill Paugussetts have been recognized by the state since 1933, but still they are not recognized as a tribe by the US Bureau of Indian Affairs.

DREAMING IN SIMSBURY

Did you know that Martin Luther King Jr. spent two formative summers in Simsbury?

The first time Martin Luther King Jr. experienced life outside the segregated South, it was in Simsbury. He spent the summers of 1944 and 1947 here, and his letters home expressed wonder in the freedom to eat in any restaurant and sit wherever he pleased on public transportation.

The summer before he entered Morehouse College in Atlanta, King joined a Morehouse-organized program that brought him to Simsbury to pick tobacco on the Cullman Brothers' tobacco farm. Students labored in the fields from 7 a.m. to 5 p.m., earning $4 a day. They lived in dormitories where King was assigned to serve drinks in the cafeteria, and he was nominated by his peers—at age 15—to lead them in worship. He wrote to his mother: "Sunday morning we had church in the dorm and I led it. I am the religious leader. I have to speak on a text every Sunday to 107 boys." He sang in the choir at First Church in Simsbury—his first time at an integrated church—and also attended services in Hartford. On his application to Crozer Theological Seminary, he wrote how he came to pursue the ministry: "The decision came about in the summer of 1944 when I felt an inescapable urge to serve society. In short I felt

In 2009, Simsbury High School students produced a short documentary titled *Summers of Freedom: the Story of Martin Luther King, Jr. in Connecticut*, which is the source for this story.

A memorial commemorating Martin Luther King Jr.'s formative summers in Connecticut, initiated by Simsbury High School students who also created a documentary on the subject, was completed in January 2021. Image courtesy of Simsbury Free Library.

MLK MEMORIAL

What: Martin Luther King Jr.'s summers in Simsbury

Where: Simsbury Free Library, 749 Hopmeadow St., Simsbury

Cost: Free

Noteworthy: The *Martin Luther King, Jr. in Connecticut Memorial* at the Simsbury Free Library was unveiled on January 18, 2021.

a sense of responsibility which I could not escape."

In their leisure time, the Morehouse students saw movies, swam in the Farmington River, and explored Hartford. In his autobiography, King reflected: "After that summer in Connecticut it was a bitter feeling going back to segregation." Connecticans can be proud to know that King's positive experiences in the state were an inspiration for his work to achieve the dream of equality for all.

I HAVE A BRIDGE TO SELL YOU

Does Greenwich have its own Brooklyn Bridge?

Generations of boaters have navigated Greenwich Harbor, admiring elegant estates with lawns rolling to private piers. One pier in particular stands out for a structure with an unmistakable resemblance to the Brooklyn Bridge.

Indeed, this pedestrian footbridge that connects the home's land with a pier was designed and built by the same company that erected one of the most famous bridges in the world, John A. Roebling's Sons Company. In addition to its renowned vehicular bridges, the company also built pedestrian suspension bridges that are now on public land from Brunswick, Maine, to Waco, Texas; the Greenwich bridge is thought to be the only one on private property.

The Brooklyn Bridge was not even 20 years old when George Pynchon joined other titans of industry in purchasing land in an exclusive Greenwich residential development called Field Point Park. A stockbroker and a champion yachtsman, he needed a functional pier and had the means to further enhance the beauty of his property with a landmark feature.

Roebling engineer Sebern A. Cooney connected Pynchon's waterfront seawall with a stone pier, completing the 175-foot bridge in 1903. Its walkway is four feet wide, the cables are one inch in diameter, and the steel towers feature decorative circles.

ROEBLING PEDESTRIAN BRIDGE

What: Mini Roebling-designed quasi-Brooklyn Bridge

Where: Private Greenwich waterfront property visible from Greenwich Harbor.

Cost: Please admire from a distance: No trespassing.

Noteworthy: In the 1920s, George Pynchon used Roebling wire in the rigging for his most famous racing yacht, the 65-foot *Istalena*.

What's thought to be the only Roebling-designed pedestrian bridge on private property can be seen from Greenwich Harbor. Photo courtesy of Marlene Pixley.

In the same era, George Parker became infamous for conning people into buying access rights to the Brooklyn Bridge, a practice that resulted in people saying to the gullible public, "And if you believe that, I have a bridge to sell you." Well, Greenwich realtors actually can sell the town's own Brooklyn Bridge, if the buyer also wants a $40 million home to go with it.

Greenwich has another connection to the Brooklyn Bridge: bluestone granite from the Byram Shore quarries was used in constructing it (and also the base of the Statue of Liberty).

A MIKVAH IN MONTVILLE

Did you hear the one about the Jewish farmers in Connecticut?

At the turn of the 20th century, one wouldn't necessarily expect to find a *mikvah* (Jewish ritual bathhouse) in Montville, but its remnants still are there, on the New England Hebrew Farmers of the Emanuel Society Synagogue and Creamery Site.

Beginning in the early 1890s, Jews who had been living in New York City tenements after emigrating from Russia and Eastern Europe began establishing farms in rural Connecticut.

Some Yankee farmers were selling their homesteads and taking advantage of incentives to settle out West, where the grass metaphorically was greener and the land literally less rocky. Aided by the Baron de Hirsch Fund, thousands of Jews found themselves in two areas of the state: Colchester, Lebanon, and Chesterfield; and Rockville, Vernon, Ellington, and Somers. The Jewish Agricultural Society (JAS) was instrumental in this Back to the Land movement, lending money and providing education and infrastructure to assist in their success. Farm agents organized much of the transition, and a publication called *The Jewish Farmer* kept the community informed.

Some farmers accepted Jewish city-dwelling paying guests in summer, and 30 small resorts also were part of the "Borscht Belt," hosting entertainers like Zero Mostel.

CONNECTICUT'S BORSCHT BELT

What: Jewish farmers

Where: Numerous towns

Cost: N/A

Noteworthy: A railroad tycoon, Baron Maurice de Hirsch (1831–1896), was a philanthropic German Jew whose support resettled thousands of persecuted Russian and Eastern European Jews in North and South America, primarily in agricultural pursuits.

Ellington's Rashall-Cantor Chicken Facility once was the largest in Connecticut, with approximately 25,000 chickens. Photo courtesy of the Ellington Historical Society.

The Jewish farmers branched out and became *shohets* (kosher butchers), feed suppliers, and chicken brokers. They worshipped in synagogues in towns such as Ellington, Lebanon, and Lisbon, and worshipped seasonally in shuls in cities like Danbury and New London.

The characterization of a Yankee can be expanded to include someone who uses a mikvah.

The JAS assisted close to 10,000 Jewish families across 15 states, including at least 5,000 in Connecticut alone.

FIRST IN FLIGHT

Did a Bridgeport man fly two years before the Wright Brothers?

Sammy Kusterer's teacher sent her to the principal's office for insisting that the Wright Brothers weren't the first to fly a plane. What did she know that the teacher didn't? Kusterer is the great-great-granddaughter of Gustave Whitehead, who at dawn on August 14, 1901 in Fairfield, unfolded the wings of his 21st attempt at a manned aircraft and flew approximately a mile at an elevation of 50 feet. Two years later, the Wright Brothers claimed the first flight.

There has been much controversy about the "First in Flight" title over the years, but recent research that includes newly digitized newspaper archives has uncovered many previously unknown sources that confirm Whitehead's claim. The *Bridgeport Herald* was the original known documented source; the writer accompanied Whitehead on the flight.

Born in Germany as Gustav Weißkopf, he built engines professionally; worked with sails, motors, and propellers; tested kites used in meteorological measurements and aerial photography; built gliders; and was chief engineer of America's first aviation organization while building his own flying crafts.

North Carolina and Ohio refute Whitehead's claim, as does the Smithsonian (which is under legal obligation to support the Wrights), but in 2013 the Connecticut General Assembly and the governor recognized Whitehead as the first to pilot a manned,

GUSTAVE WHITEHEAD

What: A Bridgeport aeronautical pioneer

Where: Fairfield Museum and History Center, 370 Beach Rd., Fairfield

Cost: Free–$5

Pro Tip: The Fairfield Museum's library holds a specialized collection of Whitehead-related books and documents, and a mini Whitehead exhibition in its foyer tells his story.

There is controversy surrounding the claim that Gustave Whitehead flew before the Wright Brothers, but many aeronautical authorities and the State of Connecticut recognize his groundbreaking achievements. Photos courtesy of Collection John Brown, www.gustavewhitehead.com.

powered, heavier-than-air aircraft on a controlled, sustained flight. A marker at Whitehead's grave in Bridgeport's Lakeview Cemetery recognizes his achievement, and a suspended model of his craft hovers over a fountain at the intersection of Fairfield Avenue and State Street Extension.

Here's hoping a future child of Kusterer's won't be sent to the principal for claiming her ancestor's aeronautical accomplishments.

Whitehead's story was the subject of a *60 Minutes* segment titled "Wright Is Wrong?" that was spurred by a 1986 test of a replica of Whitehead's aircraft, built at Bridgeport's Captain's Cove Seaport.

BACK TO THE FUTURE

Is a Connecticut scientist working on a time machine?

Ronald Mallett always liked building gadgets. He and his dad constructed crystal radios and other electronics, but when he was 10 his father died suddenly and Ronald's world stopped.

It started back up only when he read *The Time Machine* by H. G. Wells and began dedicating his life to inventing a time machine so he could see his father again.

Mallett worked in technology in the Air Force and earned a doctorate in physics from Pennsylvania State University; his thesis included studying the possibility of backward time travel using gravity.

He studied Einstein's work, building on the theory that time slows down with faster motion.

He also studied black holes, which are related theoretically to time travel. His experience with lasers at United Technologies led him to believe that it would be possible for circulating light to create a space-time loop.

A University of Connecticut physics professor since 1975, Mallett and his colleague, experimental physicist Chandra Roychoudhuri, have created a prototype for a time machine. Building it is another hurdle.

As Mallett was inspired by Wells's story, and also by the autobiographies of Sammy Davis Jr., and James Baldwin, he wrote his own memoir to encourage others. *Time Traveler: A Scientist's Personal Mission to Make Time Travel a Reality* discusses his journey overcoming poverty and racism to gain

FOR LOVE OF FAMILY

What: Time machine

Where: In the future

Cost: Millions

Noteworthy: Wells's *The Time Machine* came out in 1895, and Einstein published his theory of relativity in 1905. It's about time (pun intended) that there's progress on a time machine.

14

UConn physicist Dr. Ronald Mallett has been working on designing a time machine for several decades; he's written a book and Spike Lee has optioned his story. Photo courtesy of Goodreads.

the knowledge he needed to attempt to manipulate the space-time continuum.

If this sounds like a movie, it might be. Spike Lee optioned Mallett's memoir, but nothing has come of it yet. Maybe one day in the future, someone will transport him to see it.

Mallett's time machine would be able only to transport someone back to when the machine was switched on; ending up in, for example, ancient Egypt wouldn't be possible.

AN ISLAND RETREAT

Is there a serene sanctuary in Mystic to experience divine beauty and learn the bagpipes?

Don't mix up the weekends for a silent retreat and a piping and drumming workshop!

On an 11-acre island at the end of another island, close in distance but far in feel from downtown Mystic, lies a serene spot for contemplating God, nature, art, and sobriety. The public is welcome to come to Enders Island for Mass, to sit in the rose garden, take in the 360-degree ocean views, or join a retreat or program.

The island was gifted in 1954 to the Society of St. Edmund by Dr. Thomas Enders and Alys Van Gilder Enders, who believed that their special home would best be used by a religious organization. Mass is held daily at the chapel of Our Lady of the Assumption, and an outdoor Seaside Chapel overlooks Fishers Island Sound. There are shrines, Stations of the Cross, and a Marian grotto, but you don't need to be Catholic to appreciate the quiet, windswept beauty of the rough fieldstone buildings that blend beautifully into their rocky island setting, the two gazebos, the pergola, and the meticulously maintained gardens that provide secular settings for contemplation.

Robust programming includes the study of calligraphy, mosaics, and oil painting at the Sacred Art Institute and retreats that focus on silence, bereavement, and recovery.

Enders Island is reached via Mason's Island, where, tucked away in the Mystic River Marina, Kitchen Little serves legendary breakfasts.

A beautiful little island in Mystic is open to the public for Catholic Mass and spiritually focused day and overnight programs. Photo courtesy of Enders Island.

Adults are welcome to book independent overnight stays, but if you've ever been curious about the sacred history of bagpipes or how to introduce Gregorian chants to your congregation, you've found your people.

ENDERS ISLAND

What: Serene spiritual retreat

Where: 1 Enders Island, Mystic

Cost: Ground visits are free; program costs vary.

Pro Tip: There's a public restroom in the chapel and a gift shop in the foyer of St. Michael's Hall. Please treat this serene, spiritual setting with respect.

THE FREEMAN SISTERS AND LITTLE LIBERIA

Who was the second-wealthiest person in Bridgeport in 1883?

There was a 19th-century community on the Connecticut coast where residents sailed on whaling ships, worked on the light bulb with Thomas Edison, ran a four-story resort hotel, fought in the Civil War, and became successful entrepreneurs. They were savvy about real estate, organized a free lending library, and attended church, school, and Freemason meetings. What's remarkable about that? The residents were Black and Native American.

At a time when slavery was legal, the South End of Bridgeport was a bustling community where free people of color lived and worked, building lives and businesses. In 1821, Jacob Freeman bought a house with John Feeley. Of African and Paugussett heritage, Freeman was a community leader, and his sisters, Eliza and Mary, eventually followed him to Little Liberia (earlier known as Ethiope and Liberia) and built adjoining houses in 1848 that they rented and ultimately occupied. Eliza died two decades before Mary, whose real estate investments made her the second-wealthiest person in Bridgeport, after P. T. Barnum.

The community attracted notable residents, including Lewis Latimer, who worked with Thomas Edison and Alexander Graham Bell on the light bulb and telephone; and William Sherman, the seaman and Paugussett ancestor whose property

---

There is evidence that Little Liberia was part of the Underground Railroad, with Shinnecock tribe members transporting Blacks escaping slavery in canoes from Long Island.

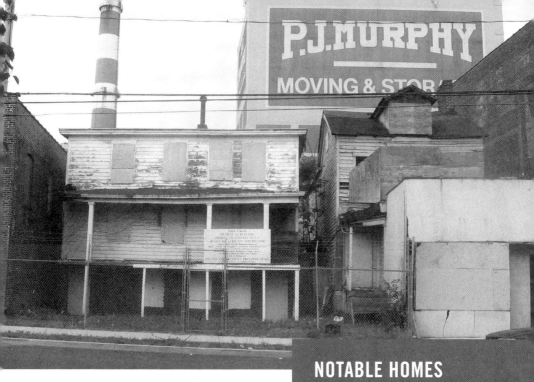

Built in 1848, the side-by-side homes of sisters Mary and Eliza Freeman are the last remnants of the groundbreaking Little Liberia neighborhood. Photo courtesy of Wikipedia, Pedro Xing.

was whittled to a quarter acre and now is a Trumbull reservation.

The agency, prosperity, and community care that Little Liberia residents demonstrated in the face of great adversity leave a legacy. The only tangible remains are two side-by-side homes that show their age but stand as a reminder of two sisters and a neighborhood that quietly upended society's views and expectations to persevere as proud survivors.

NOTABLE HOMES

What: Endangered historic homes of two high-achieving, 19th-century Black women.

Where: Mary and Eliza Freeman Houses, 352-4 and 358-60 Main St., Bridgeport

Cost: Free to drive past. They are not currently open to the public.

Noteworthy: The Freeman Houses, the oldest houses built by African Americans in Connecticut, are on the National Register of Historic Places and listed as endangered.

GATSBY IN WESTPORT

Is the Inn at Longshore Gatsby's mansion?

In 1920, after having been booted from at least one New York City hotel for hedonism, newlyweds F. Scott and Zelda Fitzgerald bought a car with the money Scott had made from *This Side of Paradise* and ended up in Westport, where they rented a cottage next to what now is Longshore Club Park.

At the time, the 175-acre property on the Long Island Sound belonged to mystery millionaire Frederick E. Lewis, who inherited the equivalent of $240 million on his 21st birthday.

Lewis flew planes, skippered yachts, drove race cars, and had stables full of Arabian horses. He threw parties that were spectacles, including one that drew 800 cars full of guests who saw a Harry Houdini show, a full circus, and many big-name entertainers of the day. John Philip Sousa even wrote music for it.

The Fitzgeralds could see across the bay, where another grand estate had a lawn that rolled to a beach and a long dock with a green light. Barbara Probst Solomon grew up on that estate and wrote a 1996 *New Yorker* article connecting the dots to Westport and the Fitzgeralds. It went largely unrecognized until Richard Webb Jr. and Robert Steven Williams took up the cause, spending years respectively researching a book and producing a documentary that provided sufficient evidence that Westport

Scott and Zelda Fitzgerald honeymooned in Westport in a cottage next to the great estate of a mystery millionaire who lived across the inlet from a mansion whose dock had a green light. Photo courtesy of Gatsby in Connecticut LLC and Alden T. Bryan.

is a setting for both of the Fitzgeralds' writings that the president of Great Neck's historical society conceded.

Find your high school copy of *The Great Gatsby* or order the movie on Amazon Prime, make yourself a gin and orange juice, and step back into the Roaring Twenties.

Literally walk in the Fitzgeralds' footsteps on a Webb-led Longshore walking tour, organized through the Westport Historical Society.

CONNECTICUT'S STONEHENGE

Why is an Airstream dangling from a steel beam?

"Sign Not in Use," reads the red sign at the entrance to Hogpen Hill Farms, setting the stage for an unusual experience. "Shut Up and Look," directs a yellow sign.

A large metal fish sways from a tree, a military tank sits on its rear end, and sunflowers look down 15 feet from a basketball-player-sized stainless steel vase. A bamboo thicket dissected with narrow paths invites exploration. In the middle of a small lake floats a giant black inflatable swan. Four sizable stainless steel arches lead the way to another field, like a giant Slinky stuck in the grass. Then, there's the Airstream trailer, dangling 31 feet overhead, and the arrangements of massive stone monoliths.

The owner of the 234-acre property created and carefully placed the 100 sculptures. Hogpen Hill Farms is Edward Tufte's private land that he opens to visitors occasionally so that they can see the sculptures in person. Tufte is all about seeing. He is a leader in data visualization and information architecture, leading seminars and writing books such as *The Visual Display of Quantitative Information* that have sold more than a million copies.

As you stroll across the rolling fields, around the lake, and along wooded paths, Tufte's creations are nearly always in view. He encourages people to walk around the sculptures and see

HOGPEN HILL FARMS

What: Private outdoor sculpture park

Where: 100 Weekeepeemee Rd., Woodbury

Cost: $80 per car

Pro Tip: Pack lunch—it's a gorgeous spot for a picnic.

At this 234-acre sculpture park you can walk around massive monoliths, a levitating Airstream trailer, a giant inflatable swan, and a bamboo maze. Photo courtesy of Anastasia Mills Healy.

how air is part of each one as a material, the same as stone, steel, and earth.

Another sign warns that "Old Words Deform New Seeing," so we will stop here.

Tufte's website explains: "The work is also installation art; the artist controls the artwork's location, shapes the surrounding land, creates platforms for views, and plants architectural evergreens nearby."

NO LUTE REQUIRED

What in the world is a trobairitz?

In 1991, the Connecticut General Assembly voted in favor of a surprising piece of legislation that resulted in the state hiring a troubadour.

The word "troubadour" evokes a medieval man in tights singing love songs to the nobles at court while accompanying himself on a lute. Connecticut's idea was a little different: "The State Troubadour serves as an ambassador of music and song and promotes cultural literacy among Connecticut citizens." The singer-songwriter in the role receives an annual stipend and commits to three public performances at major events such as The Governor's Arts Awards, Arts Day, and Connecticut Day at the Big E.

There have been 17 state troubadours, including the current one, Nekita Waller, who technically is a trobairitz—a female troubadour. During the Renaissance, there were a small number of trobairitz, who, like their male counterparts, were educated nobility who wrote poetry in a language called Occitan or Latin and influenced writers, including Dante and Petrarch.

There's no such lofty expectation now, but for consideration, the prospective troubadour/trobairitz must have composed and performed at least one song that promotes Connecticut. The person also needs to have been a full-time Connecticut resident for at least five years with the same amount of performance

Michigan, Louisiana, and North Dakota are among the other states that have been represented by an official state troubadour.

As the Connecticut State Troubadour (technically a trobairitz, a female troubadour), Nekita Waller performs at schools and public events around the state. Photo courtesy of Jessica Hill.

history, and be able to travel around the state and perform in educational and community settings.

Waller's tenure is up in 2021, so break out those lutes!

SINGING CONNECTICUT'S PRAISES

What: The official state troubadour

Where: All over the state

Cost: Free

Noteworthy: Nekita Waller made her stage debut at the Apollo Theater and has shared the stage with B.B. King and Ruben Studdard.

THE LADIES OF LITCHFIELD

Are these the most pampered bovines on the planet?

Every day is a spa day for a group of ladies in Litchfield.

Their tails are shampooed daily with Clear Choice and conditioned with Pantene Pro-V. Every day, they are brushed with steel wool and a livestock blower banishes any dust. Their coats and hooves are trimmed regularly, and a herd nutritionist keeps a watchful eye on their food. When the mercury dips, they have the option to exercise and shower indoors.

There is a sign over their accommodations that reads, "Every cow in this barn is a lady, please treat her as such." Yes, these 200 ladies are cows, but not just any cows—they are each worth more than many people's homes. These special ladies are award-winning bovines that produce "Milk Like It Used to Taste" and cheese that wins international awards.

In 1999 two then-executives of Manolo Blahnik (now they work with Sarah Jessica Parker on her own shoe and accessories brand, SJP) who knew nothing about farming purchased the property across the street from their home to save it from development. They studied the business and, with great attention to detail, have created a world-renowned dairy and made the Litchfield borough of Bantam a destination for foodies.

The milk these bovine royalty produce on the Litchfield farm is turned into ice cream and cheese and sold at Arethusa Farm

Arethusa Blue was voted the #1 blue-veined cheese in the world at the World Championship Cheese Contest in 2018.

The ladies of leisure at Arethusa Farm get very special treatment and produce exceptional-quality dairy products. Top photo by Anastasia Mills Healy. Photo on left courtesy of Arethusa Farm Dairy.

Dairy retail locations in Bantam, New Haven, and West Hartford. Also in Bantam, Arethusa al tavolo is a casual gourmet restaurant and Arethusa a mano sells pastries baked on the premises and light fare like quiche and panini made with Arethusa cheese. Arethusa also has a garden that supplies the restaurant with fresh vegetables. The ladies need their fresh veggies to keep their figures.

ARETHUSA FARM

What: Pampered cows that produce exceptional dairy products.

Where: 556 S. Plains Rd., Litchfield

Cost: Various

Pro Tip: In non-COVID-19 times, take a Saturday afternoon Open Barn Tour to meet the cows.

THE FIRST US PRESIDENT WAS A NUTMEGGER

Who was the first president of the United States?

The first president of the United States was an industrious, diplomatic, politically moderate, even-tempered man who signed the Declaration of Independence. His name was Samuel Huntington.

Huntington was president eight years before George Washington under the country's first founding document, the Articles of Confederation. He was president of the Continental Congress when the first document outlining the country's organization was ratified by all 13 colonies in 1781—this is where the founders first officially named the country the United States of America. The United States Constitution replaced the Articles of Confederation on March 4, 1789, and George Washington became president a month later.

Born in Windham (now Scotland, Connecticut), Huntington was a self-taught lawyer who represented Norwich in the state's General Assembly, became King's Attorney for the state, and served as chief justice of the Connecticut Superior Court before heading to Philadelphia, first as a delegate then as president of the

PRESIDENT HUNTINGTON

What: Technically, the first president of the United States

Where: 36 Huntington Rd. (Rte. 14), Scotland

Cost: Free

Pro Tip: The Huntington Homestead organizes special programs such as a 1786 Thanksgiving meal, meeting historic characters, and signing the Declaration of Independence with a quill pen.

President of the Continental Congress when the United States was formed, Samuel Huntington technically was the country's first president eight years before George Washington. Photo courtesy of Wikipedia, Charles Willson Peale.

Continental Congress (also known as the Confederation Congress and the United States in Congress Assembled). Welcomed by a 13-cannon salute, he returned to Connecticut in 1781 and served as governor from 1786 to his death in 1796.

Huntington was president during the American Revolution and faced many military, economic, and political challenges while leading a new country with divergent voices in a time of war. As governor of Connecticut, he worked on improving roads, building Hartford's Old State House, and establishing a permanent education fund for the state.

A National Historic Landmark, the Samuel Huntington Homestead is open to the public on a limited schedule. He is buried in the Norwichtown Cemetery.

The Huntington Homestead is part of The Last Green Valley National Heritage Corridor, a pastoral area of Connecticut and Massachusetts noted for its patriotism and important locations in the early history of the United States.

A RADIANT GLOW

Why were women in Waterbury dying in the 1930s?

Connecticut has a long history of developing and manufacturing timepieces. In 1915, Waterbury Clock Company was the largest clock maker in the United States.

After Marie and Pierre Curie discovered radium in 1898, this futuristic element was added to cosmetics and cocktails and touted as a health product. Radium gave women's cheeks a "healthy" glow, and doctors prescribed it for arthritis and other ailments.

Waterbury Clock developed timepieces with luminescent numbers that were useful for soldiers during World War I and became all the rage with consumers; young women hand-painted the dials and had fun with the new glow-in-the-dark paint, using it as nail polish.

To prevent the hairs of paintbrushes from spreading, workers put the tips in their mouths to create a point, sometimes hundreds of times a day. Earning eight cents per dial, the women worked fast, and over time, the radium-infused paint created health problems, including severe anemia, rotted teeth, spontaneous bone fractures, tissue decay, tumors, and extreme pain. Two other plants doing the same work had documented cases: 30 women died of radium poisoning in Waterbury; 41 in Orange, New Jersey; and 35 in Ottawa, Illinois, not to mention others who later developed cancer.

Eventually, Waterbury Clock quietly compensated victims in return for their silence—they couldn't talk to the press or get

---

By 1917, 300 workers produced 23,000 clocks and watches a day at Waterbury Clock, which became US Time in 1942 and Timex in 1969.

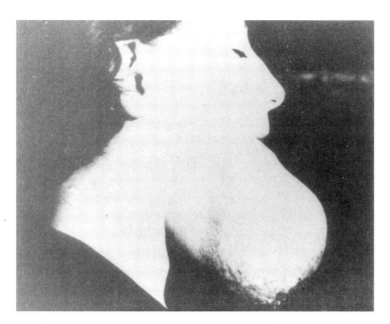

Side effects of radium poisoning include tumors, easily broken bones, rotted teeth, and extreme pain. Photo courtesy of "Deadly Glow: The Radium Dial Worker Tragedy," R. Muller. American Journal of Public Health; *April 1, 1999.*

their day in court. The afflicted were treated by a company doctor, and their cases were never reported to the health department. It was only in 2002, when the *Waterbury Observer* published an investigative feature, that the workers' stories were finally uncovered, along with the lasting impacts of the radium (it sticks around for 1,600 years) that agencies were just then attempting to remediate.

RADIUM POISONING

What: Radium poisoning in Waterbury

Where: Waterbury Clock complex, Cherry Ave. from North Elm St. to Cherry St., Waterbury

Cost: N/A

Pro Tip: Don't leave Waterbury without visiting the wonderful Mattatuck Museum, which has important art collections and historical displays.

A REFUGE IN AN ARCHIPELAGO

How can you gain access to a private archipelago?

For 200 years, an island chain has attracted homeowners who are willing to trade convenience for privacy and remarkable views.

Native Americans called them *Kuttomquash*, "beautiful sea rocks." We know them as the Thimble Islands, named for the thimbleberries that used to be abundant. Depending on how you define an island, there are between 100 and 365; approximately two dozen are inhabited. Public narrated cruises and kayak rentals are available, but to actually set foot on one, there are two options: an invitation (or a rental) from a homeowner or a trip to Outer Island.

The Thimbles are mid-coast, off Stony Creek. The farthest from shore, Outer Island, is federal land, part of the Stewart B. McKinney National Wildlife Refuge. Connecticut State University operates a scientific research facility, and a group of ecologically committed volunteers welcomes visitors and helps run educational programs.

A homeowner donated the five-acre island to the US Fish and Wildlife Service in 1995. Part of the Atlantic Flyway, it's a stop for thousands of egrets, gulls, herons, and oystercatchers that use the rocky outcrop to rest, feed, and nest. Scientists study Outer Island's flora and fauna to monitor the ecosystem, turning over rocks to count invasive crabs and netting the water to catalog creatures.

THIMBLE ISLAND WILDLIFE REFUGE

What: An island that's a National Wildlife Refuge

Where: Outer Island

Cost: Free

Pro Tip: Stop by the Stony Creek Museum to learn about this special part of Connecticut.

Outer Island, the farthest Thimble Island from shore, is a National Wildlife Refuge that's open to the public. Photo courtesy Stewart B. McKinney National Wildlife Refuge-Outer Island via Wikipedia.

The Thimble Islands are known for their private summer homes, like those on Cut in Two Island. Photo courtesy John Petrofsky.

The island allows visitors daily from May 30 to September 25, 8 a.m. to sunset; no reservation is necessary for individuals, but groups must organize in advance. So come for a Seaweed Saturday, Jellyfish Workshop, or Artists' Day, or bring binoculars and settle in on the bird-viewing platform. For a few hours, you can have your own slice of island life.

Connecticut's rare native prickly pear cactus grows in the refuge. Its yellow bloom comes in late spring or early summer and lasts for just one day.

FRIENDS, ROMANS, CONNECTICANS

Chariot race, anyone?

If you're a teenager who can recite Catullus, run like Mercury, rock a tunic, and know which North African city was Rome's enemy in the Punic Wars, you are ready for Connecticut State Latin Day.

Since 1981, middle- and high-school students studying Latin (and more recently, Greek) have been gathering annually for a day of academic, creative, and athletic competitions.

Students who like to cook compete in Iron Coquus (Iron Chef), artistic kids craft a mosaic or build the Pantheon, and *Project Runway* fans design their schools' tunics. Brainiacs show off in academic contests covering derivatives, cases, history, geography, mythology, and many more topics.

Athletes are in their element with competitions in many sports, including basketball, volleyball, canoeing, badminton, bocce, and a 2.6-mile decimated marathon. The fun-filled day culminates in two highly anticipated events: tug-of-war and chariot racing.

THE CLASSICS ARE NOT DEAD

What: Connecticut State Latin Day

Where: 43 Candee Rd., Prospect

Cost: Schools are charged a participation fee

Pro Tip: Incorporating Latin Day's annually changing theme wins points for contest entrants.

There are no non-participating spectators, but scholars with specialties like ancient astronomy and the Roman Legion are welcome to apply to give presentations.

Photo courtesy of Jim Crabb.

Chariot racing and tug of war cap off the annual Connecticut State Latin Day, a fun-filled day of athletic, scholarly, and artistic competitions for high school students studying Latin and Greek. Photo courtesy of Amy White.

Students build and decorate chariots: instead of horses, two kids pull them and there is no rider. Hey, this is Connecticut, not Carthage (the answer to Rome's enemy in the Punic Wars).

The Classical Association of Connecticut, an organization of Latin and Greek educators, organizes this event. Gratias ago tibi, magistri!

OUR OWN INDIANA JONES

Why was the man who discovered Machu Picchu governor for just one day?

The inspiration for the heroic character of Indiana Jones—a dashing American man bushwhacking through dense tropical jungles, encountering foreign cultures, and discovering archaeological treasures—can be traced to a colorful Connecticut character.

When Yale graduate Hiram Bingham III, the son of missionaries, married an heir to the Tiffany fortune in 1900, he was free economically to pursue his passions. He self-financed expeditions to Venezuela and Colombia and, after earning a PhD in South American history from Harvard, became the only professor in that subject at Yale. On a 1911 expedition to Peru, deep in the jungle of a steep mountain pass, he found Machu Picchu. Bingham removed thousands of artifacts, took hundreds of photos, and became an international celebrity. He later wrote a best seller, *Lost City of the Incas*, which became the basis for the Charlton Heston movie *Secret of the Incas*. The movie itself inspired the character of Indiana Jones, down to Indy's fedora and flight jacket.

Bingham did not go on to other archaeological adventures, but his life continued to be less than dull. He learned to fly and pursued aviation in the military during World War I, overseeing

HIRAM BINGHAM III

What: Celebrity adventurer and politician

Where: Various

Cost: N/A

Noteworthy: The character of Reverend Abner Hale in James Michener's *Hawaii* was inspired by Hiram Bingham III's grandfather, Hiram Bingham.

Photo courtesy of Harry Ward Foote, Yale University.

Hiram Bingham was an adventurer who introduced Machu Picchu to the world, an aviator who fought in World War I, and a politician who served Connecticut as lieutenant governor, governor (for one day), and senator. Photo courtesy of El Estigma de Cain.

pilot training in France and writing about it in *An Explorer in the Air Service*.

He next turned his attention to politics. On January 7, 1925, he woke up as lieutenant governor, was sworn in as governor, and attended his inauguration ball. Then, he resigned to pursue a senate seat that suddenly had been vacated by a death. He served as a United States senator until 1933, pulling stunts such as landing a blimp on the steps of the Capitol—a very Indy-worthy trick.

As a vice consul in Marseilles during World War II, Bingham's son, Hiram Bingham IV, saved 2,500 Jews, including artist Marc Chagall, from the Nazis.

IF IT FLIES, IT DIES

Where were Nike missiles hidden during the Cold War?

During the Cold War, people built bunkers, companies developed crisis plans, and kids dove under desks in school drills. With communism expanding, nations joined NATO and the Warsaw Pact, vowing to come to one another's defense in case of an attack. Countries were developing weapons and launching space missions to prove prowess.

Thankfully, the Cold War never resulted in combat on US soil, but we were prepared. To protect locations such as cities and military installations, the US Army deployed the world's first guided surface-to-air missile system, Nike Ajax, in 1954. Four years later, the US had 200 Nike Ajax sites, including 12 in Connecticut. Personnel were on call 24/7 to shoot down enemy aircraft.

Cities like Hartford and Bridgeport were protected by missile sites in West Haven, Milford, Portland, Ansonia, Cromwell, Monroe, East Windsor, Manchester, Plainville, Avon/Simsbury, Fairfield, and Westport from the mid-1950s through the early 1960s.

Most were on public land like parks and forests, and after decommissioning were adapted for use by private and military groups and/or overtaken by nature. Because the one in Portland is the only base that has not been redeveloped, it now is a State Archaeological Preserve. Both the 40-acre launch site and the radar site, operational between 1956 and 1963, are in the Meshomasic State Forest.

The Nike missile could reach 1,000 mph, travel 25 miles, and attain an altitude of 70,000 feet.

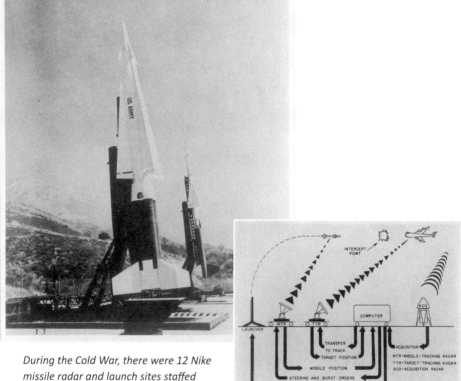

During the Cold War, there were 12 Nike missile radar and launch sites staffed 24/7 by Army personnel ready to defend the state from enemy attacks. Photos courtesy of the Library of Congress.

As technology developed, this system of ground-to-air missiles was superseded. Bases began closing in 1963, although the Cold War didn't end until the Soviet Union disbanded in 1991. These sites serve to remind citizens that our military remains vigilant in protecting the nation, even when it isn't in plain sight.

NIKE MISSILE LOCATIONS

What: Cold War missiles

Where: 12 sites including: Del Reeves Rd., Portland, Meshomasic State Forest

Cost: Free

Noteworthy: A typical Nike base housed 109 officers and enlisted personnel.

SOMETHING TO THINK ABOUT

Why are there hundreds of brains in a Yale basement?

The first Yale students who came face to face with a roomful of brains in jars in the bowels of their dorm must have been surprised, to say the least. Word got out, and it became a badge of honor to sign the white board documenting a trip to the sub-basement of E. S. Harkness Hall, thereby attaining membership in the Brain Society.

A unique record of early neurosurgery, the Cushing Brain Tumor Registry was a learning center for medical professionals for decades. It was all but forgotten and almost discarded until proponents restored the dried-out brains, organized the collection, and opened it to the public in 2010.

If you had to have brain surgery in the early 1900s you'd have wanted Dr. Harvey Cushing to hold the scalpel. Born in 1869 and educated at Yale, Harvard, and Johns Hopkins, Cushing was fascinated with the brain and became a neurosurgery pioneer with an impressive success record. An early adopter of monitoring blood pressure and anesthesia and using stems and tourniquets to curtail bleeding, Cushing operated on several hundred patients a year, documenting cases with detailed notes, photos, and specimens.

LEARNING ABOUT BRAINS

What: A room full of human brains

Where: Cushing/Whitney Medical Library, Yale School of Medicine, 333 Cedar St., New Haven

Cost: Free

Noteworthy: A colleague of Cushing's, Louise Eisenhardt, was director of the Cushing Brain Tumor Registry, the first managing editor of the *Journal of Neurosurgery*, and one of the first neuropathologists.

Dr. Harvey Cushing was a pioneer in neurosurgery, and his collections of tissue samples, medical notations, and photographs give insight into the early years of brain surgery. Photo courtesy of Terry Dagradi, Yale University.

At the Cushing Brain Center, visitors learn about the doctor's service in World War I, his artistic and athletic skills, and his Pulitzer Prize in biography. Cushing's lab coat is displayed, as are his surgical implements, Chinese acupuncture set, patient photos, and rare books.

The brains now are in a different basement—a carefully custom-designed library space. In context, they help relate the fascinating work of a medical pioneer. All are encouraged to join the Brain Society, with no sneaking around in the dark required.

A calf's liver sporting the signature of Ivan Pavlov (of Pavlov's dogs fame) is on display; Cushing demonstrated an electrosurgical tool and Pavlov signed his name with it.

THE LIGHT ON RAGGED MOUNTAIN

In the 18th century, was there a diverse community in the Barkhamsted woods?

Archaeologists were poking around the woods of the Peoples State Forest in Barkhamsted, looking for signs of prehistoric Native American encampments, when they found something unexpected. After much digging, records searches, and interviews, they pieced together a history of a community of white people, Native Americans, and African Americans living together, beginning in 1779.

This unique settlement was set in motion when a white woman, Mary Barber, married the Narragansett Indian James Chagum. They lived in the woods, away from disapproving eyes, and their community grew to include the family they started, as well as other Native Americans, Europeans, and former slaves.

Their spot by the Farmington River, near the base of Ragged Mountain, became known as the Barkhamsted Lighthouse for the glow of their hearth flames. It signaled proximity to the stagecoach stop in New Hartford for travelers on the later-developed route between Boston and Albany.

With occupations including "odd jobs" and "basket maker," descendants of the Chagums remained part of the Lighthouse Community for nearly a century. They finally dispersed completely around 1860, leaving behind 12,000 artifacts, including copper coins and fragments of plates and clay pipes.

Dr. Kenneth L. Feder, the Central Connecticut State University archaeology professor who led the investigation, wrote *A Village of Outcasts.*

When James Chagum, a Narragansett Indian, purchased land on Ragged Mountain in 1779 and raised a family with his white wife, Mary, the diverse Lighthouse community was born in the woods of Barkhamsted. Image courtesy of Coni Dubois.

The site now is a State Archaeological Preserve that's listed on the National Register of Historic Places; in the Peoples State Forest, the Nature Museum interprets this distinctive community.

LIGHTHOUSE COMMUNITY

What: Remains of a diverse 18th century community

Where: Nature Museum, Peoples State Forest, East River Rd., Barkhamsted

Cost: Free

Noteworthy: There's now a network of Lighthouse Community descendants who keep in touch.

BOYS WILL BE BOYS

How did the Boy Scouts begin?

A few minutes' walk from the parking lot of Pomerance Park in Cos Cob, a section of Greenwich, are the remains of an estate called Wyndygoul. When it belonged to Ernest Thompson Seton at the beginning of the last century, signs of vandalism kept appearing. Thinking it was in response to the fence he put up in the woods where local kids used to hang out, he invited the suspected miscreants from Cos Cob School to bring a blanket and spend Easter weekend of 1902 camping at Wyndygoul.

Around a bonfire, he spoke of loyalty, teamwork, and principles. A leading naturalist and author with a dynamic personality, Seton taught the boys about the woods and animals and spoke reverently about how Native Americans lived traditionally in communion with nature. The approximately 17 boys who canoed and slept in teepees unknowingly became the forefathers of the Boy Scouts.

Calling the group "The League of Woodcraft Indians," Seton engaged boys in athletic competitions and taught them outdoor skills. He published an outdoor instruction book, *The Birch Bark Roll of Woodcraft*, based on his *Ladies' Home Journal* articles. In 1906, while in England, Seton presented a copy to an English military hero and outdoorsman, Lord Robert Baden-Powell, who relied heavily on it for his own *Scouting for Boys*.

THE BEGINNINGS OF THE BOY SCOUTS

What: How the Boy Scouts began

Where: Pomerance Park, 101 Orchard St., Cos Cob

Cost: Free

Noteworthy: Seton was a leader in the Camp Fire Club of America, an outdoorsmen's club and conservation organization founded prior to the Woodcraft Indians, which also held meetings at Wyndygoul.

On his wooded Greenwich estate, Ernest Thompson Seton invited boys to camp in teepees, learn outdoor skills, and compete in athletic races. Photos courtesy of Library of Congress.

When Powell's American branch was founded in 1910, Seton was the first Chief Scout of the Boy Scouts of America, and he penned the first *Boy Scout Handbook*.

Around a campfire in the Greenwich woods began an organization that has taught millions of young people skills to become better members of their communities and citizens of the planet.

Founder of the Sons of Daniel Boone and author of the 1882 *The American Boy's Handy Book*, Daniel Carter Beard also was instrumental in founding the Boy Scouts of America.

BERLIN GRAFFITI

Is there a link between Berlin and an iconic movie?

Tail-fin cars parked at sleek silver diners, neon signs, bowling alleys, dance halls, drive-in theaters—this was the Berlin Turnpike in its heyday.

Developed over time to be the epitome of a modern roadway, by 1942 it was a four-lane, divided thoroughfare helping connect New Haven to Boston. A wide, 11-mile stretch lined with 200 businesses, it served a greater purpose than conveying business travelers and families. It was a destination in itself for many people in Connecticut.

Friends could meet at a hot dog stand, share an ice cream at a dairy bar, and even go to a petting zoo. The most popular pastime, though, was cruising. The Pike was a place to see and be seen, to show off a hot rod, and to drag race; its 32 gas stations earned it the nickname Gasoline Alley.

This late 1950s/early 1960s cruising culture was captured perfectly in *American Graffiti*, which fledging director George Lucas based on his experiences in Modesto, California. A Berliner was working in Hollywood at this time and reminisced with someone close to the film about parallel events that ended up in the movie.

> ### BERLIN TURNPIKE
>
> **What:** An iconic roadway
>
> **Where:** The Berlin Turnpike
>
> **Cost:** Free
>
> **Noteworthy:** At its peak, 40,000 cars a day traveled on the Berlin Turnpike.

American Graffiti earned five Academy Award nominations, gave Lucas enough standing to get *Star Wars* produced, and launched the careers of actors, including Harrison Ford.

In its prime, the Berlin Turnpike was a popular stretch to grab a bite, bowl a game, and most of all, to cruise. Photo courtesy of Berlin Historical Society.

American Graffiti takes place during one night when high school graduates cruise, go to a diner, fool around, and drag race. The characters are on the verge of losing their innocence, as is the country; the film is set in 1962, before the cultural shift and the assassinations of the 1960s. For the Berlin Turnpike, the shift came in 1965 when Interstate 91 opened and diverted traffic and business. Some vestiges of its renowned roadside architecture remain, but like the movie, it was a snapshot in time.

BEYOND THE HAND SOCK

Why are adults playing with puppets?

Students study biomechanics, commedia dell'arte, and stop-motion animation. They work with reticulated foam and buckram and become proficient with sewing machines, band saws, and drill presses. Since this program began in 1964, they've staged upwards of 500 productions, from *The Fantasticks* to *Macbeth*, and worked with performing arts groups statewide, including The Eugene O'Neill Theater Center and The Hartford Symphony; they've also collaborated with national organizations like PBS. Who are these creative, intelligent, industrious students? They're in the University of Connecticut's Puppet Arts program.

UConn is the only university in America that offers three puppetry degrees: a BFA for undergraduates and both an MA and MFA at the graduate level. Yes, you can earn a master's in puppetry. Parents might roll their eyes and ask, "What in the world do you do with a puppetry degree?" Alumni work with puppets and animation in film, television, commercials, and theme parks, and on stage. They write books, design toys, direct schools and museums, and teach. Some work with a nonprofit

PLAYING WITH PUPPETS

What: World-class instruction in the art of puppetry

Where: Ballard Institute and Museum of Puppetry, 1 Royce Cir., Ste. 101B, Storrs

Cost: Museum is free, course prices vary.

Noteworthy: Professor Frank W. Ballard started UConn's puppetry program in 1964, and it was immediately popular.

UConn's Puppet Arts programs are world-renowned and the university also has a puppetry museum. Photo courtesy of Sean Flynn Uconn Photos.

that creates films for children that address sensitive topics such as land mines and HIV in countries like Syria and Haiti.

Some of the most accomplished puppet artists in the world have academic degrees from this special program at UConn. These students have come a long way from putting socks over their hands and talking from behind their living room couches.

On UConn's campus, the Ballard Institute and Museum of Puppetry exhibits puppets from all over the world, presents events, and holds the country's foremost repository of audiovisual materials about puppetry.

HOLY MACKEREL

How did 152 concrete panels and 20,000 pieces of stained glass unintentionally come together to form a fish?

There's a stunning church in Stamford with both a floor plan and an external shape of a fish. The fish is an ancient symbol of Christianity. The architect also was responsible for the headquarters of the United Nations, the Metropolitan Opera House, and Rockefeller Center. Put all these facts together and one would reason that the fish shape was intentional, but in fact it was realized only during construction.

The First Presbyterian Church in Stamford looks so much like a fish that it is actually called the Fish Church—check its website (fishchurch.org) if you don't believe me. The form of the church was determined by its need for exceptional acoustics. "Finally we arrived at the shape of an elongated megaphone to spread the sound toward the rear. That determined the shape. The fish symbolism was discovered later. When you are finally done, people will always rationalize," architect Wallace Harrison explained in the June 1959 edition of *Journal of the AIA*.

It seems Harrison was too preoccupied to notice the fish shape, instead being focused on designing and engineering 20,000 stained glass pieces in 86 hues that were placed in 152 concrete panels and installed at 74- to 78-degree tilts. "Have you ever thought what it would be like to live inside a giant sapphire?" he asked. The soaring sanctuary has no columns or

FISH CHURCH

What: Magnificent fish-shaped church

Where: 1101 Bedford St., Stamford

Cost: Free

Pro Tip: For the full effect of the stained glass, view the sanctuary from the balcony on a sunny day.

It's hard to fathom, but Stamford's spectacular Fish Church was not intentionally designed in the shape of a fish. Photo courtesy of Robert Gregson.

Photo courtesy of Propellerheads.

buttresses, so the effects of the dazzling *dalle de verre* is exactly how he intended it, inspired by the great cathedrals of Europe, including Sainte-Chapelle in Paris.

The Fish Church was dedicated in 1958 and has inspired exclamations of "Holy Mackerel!" ever since.

The heaviest of the 56 bells in the church's 260-foot carillon is 6,820 pounds.

WAR WITH PENNSYLVANIA AND CLAIM TO CLEVELAND

Why did the states battle, and what does Wyoming have to do with it?

It could have been Cleveland, Connecticut. England's 1662 land grant for Connecticut was between the 41st and the 42nd parallels, from Narragansett Bay "to the South Sea on the West Part." Got that? Other charters overlapped or were just as vague. That is how Connecticut and Pennsylvania ended up fighting the Pennamite Wars for 30 years over 23 miles of fertile land in the Wyoming Valley of Pennsylvania, each side standing firm on opposite banks of the Susquehanna River.

A bloody 1778 massacre here became infamous. When the Western territory that became Wyoming needed a name, a politician familiar with Pennsylvania's Wyoming Valley suggested it. Later, he saw for himself that the two regions looked nothing alike, but it was too late.

In 1786, the Connecticut settlers gave up the Pennsylvania-area land claim, except for what still is called the Western Reserve: 120 miles along Lake Erie that includes Cleveland. The lead surveyor was Moses Cleaveland from Canterbury, Connecticut. Fifty people settled in "New Connecticut" and Cleaveland went home, never returning to the Connecticut

With the Connecticut militia in the Wyoming Valley sparse from fighting the British elsewhere, on July 3, 1778, 500 Pennamite Loyalists, British soldiers, and Native American warriors killed most of the Yankees.

Connecticut fought a 30-year battle with Pennsylvania over a strip of land where, on July 3, 1778 Yankees were massacred, although the fighting didn't end until 1799. The Wyoming Massacre, *F.O.C. Darley, ca. 1905. Courtesy of Library of Congress.*

Western Reserve city that was named for him (and which somehow lost an "a").

The western part of the reserve was given to the residents of Fairfield, Danbury, and New London, whose homes were destroyed during the Revolution. There's a Trumbull County now outside of Cleveland, place names like Norwich and New London, and town greens with white-steepled churches.

The Pennamite Wars finally ended in 1799 with a compromise: the Connecticut settlers could keep their land, but it was now no longer part of Connecticut.

WARRING WITH THE WEST

What: Connecticut's western land claims

Where: Pennsylvania and Ohio between the 41st and 42nd parallels

Cost: Free

Noteworthy: Wyoming, Pennsylvania, has held an annual Fourth of July commemoration of the Battle of Wyoming since 1878. Near Wilkes-Barre, the Wyoming Monument marks the mass grave of the Connecticut settlers who died in the massacre.

IRANISTAN: NOT A FORMER SOVIET STATE

What the heck was a Moorish castle doing in Bridgeport?

The Klein Memorial Auditorium is a wonderful building, but imagine on its site in 1848, P. T. Barnum's extraordinary "Oriental Villa" Iranistan, surrounded by 17 bucolic acres.

In his travels with Tom Thumb, Barnum had visited the Royal Pavilion in Brighton, England, and was so taken by its domes and minarets that he instructed his architect, Leopold Eidlitz, to lift some of its elements for his own home.

Punctuated by statuary, a grand external staircase led to a wildly exotic three-story building, each floor lined with ornate arches. Numerous smaller onion domes surrounded an enormous central one. Measuring 124 feet long and 90 feet tall, this ornate spectacle housed a ballroom and billiard room and had the luxury of indoor plumbing, including both hot and cold running water. It took 500 workers two years to erect this fanciful, $100,000 palace, and the newspapers reported that 1,000 people attended the housewarming party.

Iranistan became a tourism magnet, with the curious traveling to lay their eyes on such an unusual building. Barnum kept the grounds open to the public so people could stroll the gardens, with their fountains, trees, and planted urns. The property also had a greenhouse, stable, carriage house, and animals. In true

Barnum modeled Iranistan on Brighton's extravagant Royal Pavilion, King George IV's pleasure palace, which was completed in 1823 after 35 years of additions and still stands today.

P.T. Barnum's first home was a fanciful Moorish stunner, the likes of which had never been seen in the US. Photo courtesy of The Barnum Museum, Bridgeport, Connecticut.

Barnum fashion, an Indian elephant plowing a field became an occasional publicity stunt to wow passengers on the nearby train, enticing them to visit his American Museum in New York.

While it was unoccupied, Iranistan burned to the ground in 1857. Barnum went on to build three successive homes in Bridgeport, but none nearly as fanciful as his first grand gesture of architectural showmanship.

BRIDGEPORT PALACE

What: The greatest home of the Greatest Showman

Where: Current site of the Klein Memorial Auditorium, 910 Fairfield Ave., Bridgeport

Cost: N/A

Noteworthy: Bridgeport's Barnum Museum is undergoing renovation and object restoration, following a tornado and multiple hurricanes.

THE GOLDEN AGE OF COMICS ON THE GOLD COAST

Which famous comic artists lived in Fairfield County?

Not so long ago, the "funnies" were an essential part of every weekend, if not every day. Strips were chuckled over by families and discussed at work around the country. When the Hearst publishing company once circulated 1,000 Sunday papers without the comics as a test, 880 out of 1,000 recipients complained (only 45 did so in a similar experiment when the news section was left out).

Due to its proximity to Manhattan publishers, Fairfield County found itself home to around 100 of America's most famous comic-strip artists, cartoonists, and illustrators, many of whom socialized at golf outings and parties over many, many cocktails.

From the 1950s to the 1990s, the self-described Connecticut School included Ernie Bushmiller (*Nancy*) in Stamford and Dik Browne (*Hägar the Horrible*) in Wilton; Stan Drake (*Blondie*), Bud Sagendorf (*Popeye*), and Leonard Starr (*Little Orphan Annie*) in Westport; and Mort Walker (*Beetle Bailey*, *Hi and Lois*), Tony DiPreta (*Joe Palooka*), and John Cullen Murphy (*Prince Valiant*) in Greenwich.

Their work was known around the world, but not many could have recognized these immensely talented artists around

YUKKING IT UP

What: Comic artist royalty in Fairfield County

Where: Fairfield County

Cost: N/A

Pro Tip: To learn more, read Cullen Murphy's book, *Cartoon County*.

In the center, wearing a hat, Mort Walker celebrates his 40th birthday in 1963 at the Milbrook Club in Greenwich surrounded by fellow comic strip artists, cartoonists, and illustrators. Photo courtesy of the Mort Walker estate.

town. They were normal guys who stayed home and drew all day in rooms sometimes decorated with an army helmet (Mort Walker) or a Viking helmet (Dik Browne).

Hats off to the Connecticut School and the golden age of comics.

In 1974, Mort Walker opened the Museum of Cartoon Art in Greenwich (now closed). The Barker Character and Cartoon Museum in Cheshire has 80,000 objects, mostly toys and dolls.

WILLIMANTIC ROCKS

Why is the DJ wearing green tights and flippers?

Kids wave tiny American flags, and grandparents in folding chairs line Main Street wearing red, white, and blue. There's a flotilla of fire trucks and antique cars, politicians smile, and people wave from floats. What's missing from this Fourth of July parade? Marching bands. Instead, parade participants and spectators bring their own radios and tune into WILI at 1400 AM or 95.3 FM. Welcome to the largest and longest-running Boom Box Parade, first held in Willimantic in 1986.

It all started when Kathy Clark couldn't find a marching band. She suggested that the local radio station play marching band music and people could tune in on their boom boxes (which have since gone the way of cassette tapes). It worked, and everyone had so much fun that a tradition was born.

All are welcome to join the festivities, and there's no official theme. Men in a rowboat wearing tricorn hats have posed as Washington crossing the Delaware, and a "precision drill team" has brandished power drills. Participation points go to the Haggertys, whose familial formations span several blocks, and The Traveling Fish Head Club of Northeast Connecticut, which shows up every year dressed as one big fish.

Then, there are the frogs. A frog as the Sphinx, as Batman, as a mermaid, and one riding a bicycle. Frogs are the symbol of the town, and the Boom Box Parade Grand Marshal dressed in green tights and flippers one year. WILI's morning man since

Other unique Connecticut parades include the Bernese Mountain Dog Parade in Greenwich on Columbus Day and the Moosup Victory over Japan Parade in August.

DJ and Boom Box Parade Grand Marshal Wayne Norman pays homage to Willimantic's famous frogs, and a fire-breather enthralls the crowd at the annual parade. Photo courtesy of Lynn Moebus.

Photo courtesy of Peter Polomski.

1970, Wayne Norman, also has perched on a huge Boom Box dressed as the "King of Willimantic" and pulled the world's largest boom box on rollerblades.

Everyone loves a good marching band, but nothing tops a boom box parade.

MARCHING TO THE BEAT

What: A boom box parade

Where: Windham

Cost: Free

Pro Tip: Participants don't need to register; just gather at Jillson Sq. at 9 a.m. on July 4 wearing red, white, and blue, and blasting WILI.

20,000 LEAGUES UNDER THE CONNECTICUT RIVER

How did David Bushnell become the Father of Submarine Warfare in 1776?

At the end of Main Street by the town dock in postcard-perfect Essex, the Connecticut River Museum displays something really fascinating: a fully interactive replica of the world's first submarine.

When the American Revolution was in its infancy, David Bushnell knew that the scrappy Yankees had to figure out how to outsmart the more powerful and experienced British forces. The 36-year-old Yale student was working on the puzzle of both how to create an underwater explosion and also how to deliver it to an enemy vessel, safely and undetected.

With clockmaker compatriots, Bushnell successfully developed a remotely detonating underwater incendiary device using a clockwork timer, gunpowder, and musket flint. In 1776, to deliver the mechanism, he built a one-person wooden submersible that was human-powered. The operator used propellers rotated with a hand crank and a foot-powered treadle (like the pedal used in spinning wheels at the time), and let water in and out for ballast.

Named *The Turtle*, this first wooden submersible, which George Washington called "an effort of genius," ultimately was unsuccessful in its mission but paved the way for the development of the submarine. Bushnell's underwater mines,

David Bushnell's brother was to pilot *The Turtle* since he was a strong farmer, but he fell ill, so Ezra Lee of Lyme carried out the first mission.

David Bushnell invented this submarine called The Turtle *to deliver an underwater mine in 1776. Photo courtesy of the Connecticut River Museum.*

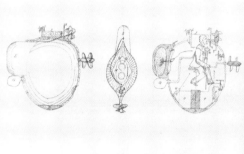

Photo courtesy of Library of Congress.

on the other hand, did detonate, and he is known now as the Father of Submarine Warfare.

Over in Groton, the Submarine Force Museum also has a replica of *The Turtle* and another of Connecticut's submarine claims to fame: the much mightier *USS Nautilus*. The first nuclear-powered submarine launched in 1954, and over its 25 years of service shattered all previous speed and distance records and traveled half a million miles.

THE FIRST SUBMARINE

What: Submarine firsts

Where: Connecticut River Museum, 67 Main St., Essex

Submarine Force Museum, 1 Crystal Lake Rd., Groton

Cost: Connecticut River Museum: Free–$10

Submarine Force Museum: Free

Pro Tip: In Essex, check out the restaurant and bar at the Griswold Inn, the oldest continuously operating inn in the country.

WOULD YOU LIKE A TOUR OF HELL?

What was life like in America's first state prison–which also happened to be an abandoned copper mine?

If you were a colonial leader in the 1700s, needed a place to house criminals, and wanted to save money, an abandoned copper mine would be a dream come true. Take the shaft ladder away, and the prisoners are stuck in the tunnels. You don't even need guards. Well, that's what they thought. . . .

The very first Newgate Prison inmate in 1773 escaped 18 days after being left alone, 75 feet underground. It's assumed that someone threw a rope down for him. After a guard house was built and staffed one year later, all the prisoners escaped by burning it down. In 1782 they pulled the same trick; the next guard house was made of stone and brick. About ten percent of prisoners disappeared in the 54 years it served as a prison. Well, this was the first state prison in the colonies—they were obviously figuring it all out.

As many as 60 inmates lived in an approximately 300-square-foot area with no light source other than an occasional beam of daylight. It was always cold (52 degrees) and damp, if not wet. No one bathed, there weren't toilet facilities, and "armies of fleas, lice, and bedbugs covered every inch of the floor which itself was covered in 5 inches of slippery, stinking

NEWGATE PRISON

What: America's first chartered copper mine and state prison

Where: 115 Newgate Rd., East Granby

Cost: Free

Pro Tip: There's a good virtual tour on the prison's YouTube channel.

America's first state prison was a cold, wet, abandoned copper mine with no bathroom and plenty of vermin. Photo courtesy of the Old New-Gate Aerial, Capture LLC, 2020.

filth," as an inmate noted in his 1854 autobiography. Sounds perfectly pleasant.

Over time, prison officials built aboveground housing, as well as workshops where inmates produced nails and barrels and milled grain with human horsepower.

The prison closed in 1827 and has been a visitor attraction almost ever since—because who wouldn't want to head deep underground and envision life in what was known as "Hell"?

The prisoner list reveals that many were thrown below for the crime of being a Tory and that several women were tossed in the mix over the years.

NAZIS GET NIMBYED

How did Southbury repel a camp for 10,000 Nazi sympathizers?

It seems preposterous now, but in the years leading up to World War II, there was a network of 20 Nazi youth and training camps around the United States, where American children and adults participated in drills, marches, ceremonies, and social activities.

In the 1930s, a quarter of all Americans had German ancestry; the German American Bund appealed to their Teutonic pride and sought support for Hitler's ideology. There were camps in Yaphank, Long Island, and Andover, New Jersey, but not in Southbury. In 1937, the town got wind that Wolfgang Jung had purchased 178 acres in Kettletown to build the largest Nazi training camp in the country.

In response, the rural town of 1,500 formed its first zoning commission and voted to allow only farming on the property and to prohibit training by any group other than the US Armed Forces. The town also cleverly arrested two Bund members for cutting down trees—they were working on a Sunday in violation of the state's blue laws. While legal proceedings were in motion, the Bund continued building the camp, and the organization's national leader, Fritz Kuhn, drove his black Mercedes to inspect the site that was going to accommodate 10,000 people. The FBI had its eye on Kuhn, and in 1939 agents convicted him of embezzling Bund funds. The US eventually revoked his

---

SAYING NO TO THE NAZIS

What: Southbury halts a Nazi camp

Where: Georges Hill Rd., Southbury

Cost: N/A

Pro Tip: Southbury filmmaker Scott Sniffen produced a 2012 documentary, *Home of the Brave*, which in 38 minutes unfolds this story through primary sources and interviews.

In the 1930s, the German American Bund organized marches and rallies like the one shown here in Manhattan and ran 20 US training camps for Nazi sympathizers; one was foiled in Southbury (seen at right circa 1940). Photo courtesy of the New York World Telegram via the Library of Congress.

Photo courtesy of the Library of Congress.

citizenship and deported him to Germany. Jung sold the land on Georges Hill Road in 1940.

NIMBY, by the way, stands for "Not in My Backyard."

The number of Bund members in 70 regional divisions across the country is unclear, but a 1939 rally at Madison Square Garden in Manhattan was attended by 20,000 people.

SPOOKY FUN

Why is there creepy organ music coming from an industrial warehouse in Plainville?

Believe your GPS when it takes you into an eerily quiet industrial area in the dark of night. The spooky lead-up to The Witch's Dungeon Classic Movie Museum is apropos. In this unassuming building in an unassuming town is a Hollywood-worthy small collection of costumes, props, and memorabilia from classic monster movies.

The son of a painter and a costume designer and the great-nephew of the first cinematic lycanthrope (the headliner of the 1935 movie *Werewolf of London*), Cortlandt Hull was a creative kid who was fascinated by monster movies. At the age of 13 in 1966, Hull started a Halloween attraction in his Bristol neighborhood by putting his monster models and life-size characters on display, enhanced by the costumes and backgrounds his parents contributed.

WITCH'S DUNGEON

What: A tribute to classic monster movies

Where: 103 E. Main St., Plainville

Cost: $4–$8

Pro Tip: Arrive before opening to cut down time spent in line.

Over time, Hull became a professional artist in the field. He reached out to special effects artists, make-up artists, and actors who worked on the films he loved, and his sheer enthusiasm resulted in donations of life casts of the actors, props, and costumes that were in films like *Creature from the Black Lagoon* and *House of Wax*. He's created atmospheric tableaux with 22 life-size figures of Bela Lugosi, Boris Karloff, Lon Chaney, Vincent Price, and others from the golden age of horror and sci-fi cinema, complete with organ music.

The museum grew, changed locations, drew national attention, and received support from the museum's subjects.

Cortlandt Hull's collection includes life casts, costumes, and props from classic monster movies including Dracula, Frankenstein, *and Jean Cocteau's iconic 1946 French film* La Belle et La Bête (Beauty and the Beast). *Photos on top and at left courtesy of The Witch's Dungeon.*

Actors, including Vincent Price and Mark Hamill, provided tour recordings, and the children of Boris Karloff and Bela Lugosi greeted visitors.

Now, this loving tribute to classic monster films is the longest-running Halloween attraction in the country.

The museum also displays props from movies including *Indiana Jones*, *Planet of the Apes*, and *Mars Attacks!*

O LITTLE TOWN

What do nuns, Elvis, and Santa have in common?

"Connecticut's Christmas Town" is the site of America's first theological school, an abbey, and an iconic small-town holiday celebration. Thousands of people come every year to tour the Bellamy-Ferriday House and Garden, hear the nuns of the Abbey of Regina Laudis sing Gregorian chants, marvel at the abbey's 300-year-old Neapolitan crèche, and take part in the Christmas Town Festival. Another big draw is mailing Christmas cards at the post office, so friends and relatives can receive holiday greetings postmarked Bethlehem. Bethlehem postal workers go above and beyond: Every year since 1938 the town has created a special holiday-themed stamp called a cachet that adds extra cheer to the nearly 200,000 pieces of mail that this town of 3,607 processes between Thanksgiving and Christmas.

BETHLEHEM

What: A small town with big Christmas spirit

Where: Town Green, Junction of Rtes. 61 & 132, Bethlehem

Cost: Free

Noteworthy: Fulbright Scholar Mother Noella Marcellino, who is featured in Michael Pollan's documentary, *Cooked*, applies her PhD in microbiology to crafting artisanal cheese.

Every December since 1981 (except for 2020), the Christmas Town Festival has included activities such as carol singing, a parade, food and crafts, a Roaming Railroad and hayride, face painting, a 5K race, and musical entertainment. Santa lights the 85-foot Christmas tree on the town green and stays for photos.

Where do nuns and Elvis fit in? Dolores Hart played Elvis Presley's love interest in *Loving You* and *King Creole* and also was in *Where the Boys Are*. Usually, cloistered nuns do not have movies with Elvis on their resumes, so it surprised the world when Mother Dolores Hart joined The Abbey of Regina Laudis

The place to be during Christmastime is Bethlehem, which mails thousands of holiday cards with special stamps and holds a Christmas festival, complete with sleigh rides and crafts. Photo courtesy of Dan Polansky.

Image courtesy of George Murdock.

in 1966. On a 400-acre working farm, the nuns tend heritage cattle and make award-winning cheese, in addition to chanting the Mass daily and praying full Divine Office. This is one small town with big Christmas spirit.

The Metropolitan Museum of Art restored the abbey's crèche, which is located fittingly in a barn and is a sister to the one the museum displays every year.

THERE'S SOMETHING ABOUT AMY

What Cary Grant movie was inspired by a shocking Windsor headline?

Amy Archer-Gilligan was an eldercare pioneer, but do not follow her business model. When she lived in Newington, she cared for the elderly owner of a house in return for free room and board. This gave her the idea to turn his home into Sister Amy's Nursing Home for the Elderly, which she ran after the owner died, until his heirs sold the home in 1907.

She moved to Windsor and operated The Archer Home for Elderly People and Chronic Invalids, charging residents a weekly fee or a $1,000 lifetime option—and that's where it gets tricky.

The alacrity at which residents were dying prompted a *Hartford Courant* obituary writer to investigate poison registers. He discovered that, citing rats and bedbugs, Archer-Gilligan had been buying arsenic. After the newspaper found a pattern in the residents' causes of death, state police exhumed bodies and found arsenic.

This mother and active church member was sentenced to life in prison in 1919 and died at the Connecticut General Hospital for the Insane in Middletown in 1962.

Inspired by Archer-Gilligan's story, the hit play *Arsenic and Old Lace* opened on Broadway in 1941 and became a 1944 Frank Capra movie starring Cary Grant. It's still a popular play, with stage revivals in New York and London and in smaller theaters around the world.

Archer-Gilligan was twice a widow, and she "lost" 60 residents—48 of whom died in the five years before she was caught.

"The Archer Private Home" for Elderly People, Windsor, Conn.

ARSENIC AND OLD LACE

What: Homicidal nursing home proprietor

Where: Windsor Historical Society, 96 Palisado Ave., Windsor

Cost: Free–$8

Noteworthy: Archer-Gilligan's case prompted oversight of eldercare facilities in Connecticut.

Amy Archer-Gilligan poisoned residents of her nursing home, inspiring the Broadway play and movie Arsenic and Old Lace. *Photos courtesy of Windsor Historical Society, Windsor, Connecticut.*

71

FRISBIE!

What do pies have to do with Frisbees?

Workers goofing off in a Bridgeport pie factory led to the creation of the Frisbee. William Frisbie started his pie business in 1871, and by the 1920s he was selling 50,000 pies a day. To blow off steam at lunchtime, workers would throw the pie tins back and forth. People tossing flying discs can be traced to ancient Greeks and the discus, but now players shouted "Frisbie!" as a heads-up. The company name was stamped on the pie tins, so when the pastime spread from local schoolkids and Yale students to other East Coast college communities, the name stuck.

Separately, Californian Fred Morrison also enjoyed throwing baking tins, made one out plastic, and sold it as a Pluto Platter. Wham-O hired him and called the disc Frisbee, capitalizing on the name recognition but changing the spelling slightly to avoid legal issues.

Other companies jumped on the bandwagon, and today more than 100 million flying discs have been sold in 70 countries. There's now a World Flying Disc Federation, a sports organization that governs the sport of flying discs, including Ultimate, Beach Ultimate, Disc Golf, Freestyle, Guts, and Overall.

Back in Connecticut, the Frisbie Pie Company went out of business in 1959, but a Fairfield resident brought it back to life in 2016. Dan O'Connor had collected Frisbie pie tins and played

O'Connor uses more fruit and fruit juice than in the original recipes for his four-inch apple, blueberry, and cherry pies.

The Frisbie Pie Company, whose pie tins inspired the Frisbee, shuttered in 1959 after being in business for nearly a century; it was resurrected in 2016 when a flying disc enthusiast found old company recipes at an estate sale. Photo courtesy of Dan O'Connor, Frisbie Pie Company archives.

FRISBIE PIES

What: The rebirth of a pie company that launched a toy craze

Where: Various

Cost: $1.50–$1.99

Pro Tip: To find a retailer from Westport to Orange that sells Frisbie Pie Company's mini pies, go to https://www.frisbiepie.com/where-to-buy.

Ultimate Frisbee and disc golf. When he spotted handwritten Frisbie Pie Company recipe books and photographs at an estate sale, he couldn't resist acquiring the license and distribution rights. Wave if you see the replica of a 1936 Frisbie truck—it's probably O'Connor hand-delivering the pies that started a worldwide craze.

RIBBIT!

Why is Willimantic obsessed with frogs?

One can't help but notice that Willimantic has a healthy obsession with frogs. Four 2,000-pound frogs, 12 feet tall from snout to froggy foot, survey traffic crossing a bridge over the Willimantic River. Nicknamed the Frog Bridge, Thread City Crossing uses giant spools of thread to symbolize the town's legacy as a major thread producer; the frogs refer to a legend that reaches back to the French and Indian War.

In the mid-1700s, residents were awoken by strange sounds and assumed Native Americans were attacking. Panicked, they fled into the woods, but the attack never came. The next morning, thousands of frogs, dead from drought, explained the ruckus.

The mill pond where the frogs were found now is called Frog Pond; frogs have appeared on currency and been etched on high school rings. Smaller frog statues pop up around town; one wearing a tricorn hat is labeled Nathan Hale, after the Connecticut state hero who was born in nearby Coventry.

Leo Jensen of Ivoryton sculpted the whimsical bridge-dwelling amphibians from bronze, expecting that they'd become greener over time. Residents ensure they're dressed for the weather, wrapping them in red scarves at holiday time. The town must have Harry Potter fans, too: the frogs have been known to each sport a scarf from a different Hogwarts house. More recently they've been spotted wearing face masks.

Centerbrook Architects designed the bridge; Jozef Witkowski cast the sculptures in Bridgeport and produced quarter-size casts for ribbity garden sculptures.

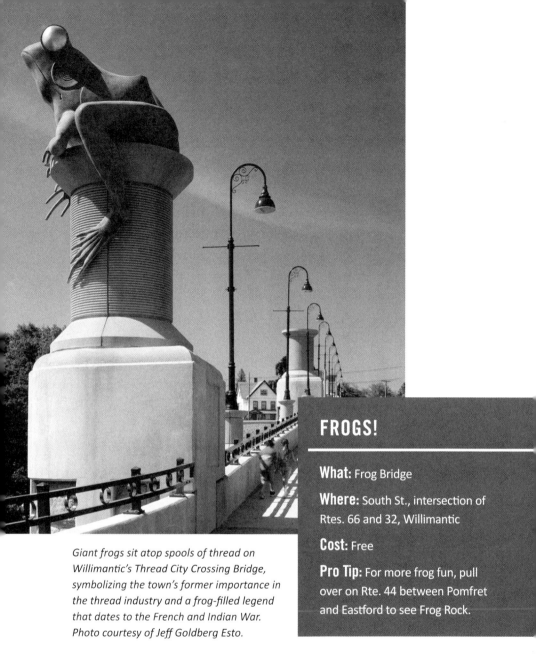

Giant frogs sit atop spools of thread on Willimantic's Thread City Crossing Bridge, symbolizing the town's former importance in the thread industry and a frog-filled legend that dates to the French and Indian War. Photo courtesy of Jeff Goldberg Esto.

FROGS!

What: Frog Bridge

Where: South St., intersection of Rtes. 66 and 32, Willimantic

Cost: Free

Pro Tip: For more frog fun, pull over on Rte. 44 between Pomfret and Eastford to see Frog Rock.

All in all, they seem pretty pleased with themselves and their station; you can sometimes catch a glint in their eyes (or maybe it's the gold leaf).

YOU CAN GO HOME AGAIN

What does Cornwall have to do with Hawaii?

Way before resorts lined the coast of the Big Island, a boy Connecticut would come to know as Henry Obookiah (born 'Ōpūkaha'ia) was orphaned in the 1796 Hawaiian civil war Battle of Kaipalaoa, and later witnessed an aunt thrown from a cliff for angering a chief.

When he spotted the China trading ship *Triumph* in Kealakekua Bay, he swam out to it. By the time he reached New Haven after a year circumnavigating the globe, he had learned English. A relative of Yale's president saw Obookiah crying on campus, frustrated because he wanted an education, and took him in. In the throes of the religious revival known as the Second Great Awakening, Obookiah lived with and was tutored at the homes of Yale president, the Reverend Dr. Timothy Dwight, and the Reverend Samuel Mills of Torringford. He converted to Christianity, and expressed a desire to return to Hawaii as a missionary.

Obookiah inspired the founding of the Foreign Mission School in Cornwall, which educated 100 students of color, many Hawaiian and Native American. He created the first formal writing system for the Hawaiian language, using the dictionary of West Hartford-born Noah Webster as a guide. With this bridge between the two

HENRY OBOOKIAH

What: Cornwall's legacy in the American settlement of Hawaii

Where: Henry Obookiah's reconstructed grave marker, Cornwall Cemetery, Cornwall

Cost: Free

Noteworthy: Harriet Beecher Stowe met Obookiah as a child and always remembered him; her father, Rev. Lyman Beecher, delivered a sermon at his funeral.

languages and his posthumously published memoir, he paved the way for missionaries in Hawaii (including Hiram Bingham).

Obookiah died of typhoid in Cornwall in 1818, but the story doesn't end there. In 1992, a descendant of Obookiah awoke in the middle of the night and knew she had to bring his remains home. The final resting place of this bright, charismatic young man, who is credited with bringing Christianity to Hawaii—and with it American education and ultimately statehood—now overlooks Kealakekua Bay. A plaque at his Cornwall gravesite records his wish: "Oh, how I want to see Hawaii!"

When the Foreign Mission School was recognized as a National Historic Landmark, descendants of its students and the Yale and Cornwall communities gathered to celebrate and discuss its complicated legacy.

HOW TO MAKE $4 BILLION FROM TEAPOT LIDS AND SPARE BOLTS

Why should you know the name George Coy?

When Alexander Graham Bell presented his invention in New Haven in 1877, a local telegraph office manager, George Coy, jumped at the chance to open his own franchise.

The following year, Coy devised the world's first telephone exchange by fashioning a switchboard from teapot lid handles, carriage bolts, and bustle wires. Covering Blackrock to Bridgeport, the District Telephone Company of New Haven kicked off on January 28, 1878, with 21 subscribers (it could have handled 64). Before this, telephone calls could only be placed between pairs of connected phones.

Three weeks later, the world's first public telephone company published the world's first telephone directory, which contained 50 names.

The company kept adding exchanges, and with its expansion to Massachusetts called itself the Southern New England Telephone Company (SNET). Its original building at Chapel and State streets was demolished in 1973.

In Hartford, above eye level at the busy intersection of Main Street and Central Row, a plaque marks another contribution to telephone history. In 1889, on the ground level of the Hartford Trust Company, a mechanic named William Gray installed the

An 1883 photo shows a Hartford switchboard at Main Street and Central Row that required six operators. Photo courtesy of Archives and Special Collections at the Thomas J. Dodd Research Center, University of Connecticut Library.

world's first coin-operated public telephone. With the backing of his former Pratt & Whitney boss, Amos Whitney, he started a company that made nascent phones available to the masses.

The pay phone was useful for generations—and for Superman—but Coy's work had more lasting impact. Bell's company became American Telephone and Telegraph (AT&T) and didn't part ways with SNET until 1984. The companies were reunited briefly when, in 1998, SBC Communications bought both SNET (for $4.4 billion) and AT&T. Now, the former SNET is part of Frontier Communications. Not bad for some found objects, a sharp mind, and an entrepreneurial spirit.

There were no phone numbers in the first telephone directory, which listed 50 subscribers, including the president of the phone company and two horse stables.

IF THESE WALLS COULD TALK

Who were the notable residents of this Greenwich house?

There's a home in Greenwich that has many stories to tell, beginning with its location in a neighborhood nearly lost to history. The area around Round Hill Road and Horseneck Brook is marked on maps of the 1800s as "Colored Settlement" and "Hangroot," probably due to the practice of hanging vegetables from the ceilings of root cellars. Free people of color settled there in the early 1800s and owned land and homes. Allen Green, a free Black man, purchased the land in 1839 and built the house in 1845.

The painter John Henry Twachtman, a founding member of the Cos Cob American Impressionist art colony, bought the home in 1890. He and fellow painters including Theodore Robinson and Childe Hassam used his home, his children, and the surrounding landscapes as subjects. It was an affordable, gentrifying neighborhood—the Rockefellers recently had purchased land nearby—and he made improvements to his house, including adding a portico that his friend, the noted architect Stanford White, possibly designed.

Jim Henson and his family lived in this house between 1964 and 1971. At the 2017 annual meeting of the Greenwich Historical Society, daughter Cheryl Henson recalled, "It was an ideal setting for a young family. An old home full of nooks and

Jim Henson built a miniature model of this family home, and the whole Henson family handmade furniture and décor for this special dollhouse.

Built by a free Black man, Allen Green, in 1845, this house later was inhabited by American Impressionist John Henry Twachtman and famed puppeteer Jim Henson. My House, *no date, oil on canvas by John Henry Twachtman. Photo courtesy of Yale University Art Gallery.*

crannies, back stairs . . . an old barn . . . a place full of history and story bordered by a forest and a wonderful babbling brook." While living there, the Henson clan grew to include five children and six cats, plus other pets and many fuzzy monsters. In the spring of 1969, before the first episode of *Sesame Street* aired, Jim treated lucky North Street School students to a performance that included Kermit and Rowlf.

A HOUSE WITH HISTORY

What: A Greenwich home with a fascinating history

Where: Private home on lower Round Hill Rd., Greenwich

Cost: Free to drive past

Pro Tip: This is a private home on a busy street.

WILD HORSES COULDN'T GET ME TO ...

Great, but can he do a back flip?

King and Queen were brother and sister. That's not the beginning of a Dark Ages saga; these are the white horses that dove from a 50-foot platform at Bristol's Lake Compounce in the early 20th century. Other horses jumped into Lake Compounce, too. Reno Guerrette from Newington trained the horse pictured here, probably circa 1911 and later than King and Queen. Lake Compounce holds the title of the oldest continually operating amusement park in the US. It's been open every summer since 1846, but J. W. Gorman's High Diving Horses are long gone.

Diving horses also wowed the crowds at the Golden Spur Amusement Park in East Lyme, where the equines ascended a ramp and leapt from a 20-foot tower. Open from 1905 to 1924, the Golden Spur attracted crowds with a merry-go-round, fun house, boating, and an island Japanese tea house, complete with pagoda.

Connecticut was not the only state to showcase diving horses. King and Queen logged many miles with J.W. Gorman, hitting amusement parks and fairs throughout the US and Canada. Other equine divers also showed up, most famously in Atlantic City, where the blind Sonora Carver plunged 40 feet riding John the Baptist into a 12-foot tank of water. Disney's 1991 film, *Wild Hearts Can't Be Broken*, is based on her story.

TAKE A DIVE

What: Diving horses

Where: Lake Compounce, 185 Enterprise Dr., Bristol

Cost: Free–$48.99

Pro Tip: Six stories high, Lake Compounce's Venus Vortex water slide, next to the lake that used to feature diving horses, will be ready for the 2021 season.

In Connecticut, diving horses were an attraction at Lake Compounce and the Golden Spur Amusement Park in the early 1900s; they only recently ended their runs in other neighboring states. Photo courtesy of Bristol Historical Society.

Horses kept jumping off Steel Pier until 1978, and it was only recently that the last known diving horse anywhere retired from the Magic Forest amusement park in Lake George, which still has a diving act (but these days, its stars now walk on two legs).

People who worked with diving horses are on record swearing that the horses were never forced to jump, and that it is something they did naturally and enjoyed.

GREEN ACRES

What green spaces in Connecticut did the father of landscape architecture design?

Best known for designing Central Park with Calvert Vaux, Frederick Law Olmsted was from Connecticut and is responsible for many green spaces in the state.

One of America's most highly regarded and best-known landscape architects, Frederick Law Olmsted Sr., was born in Hartford, spent time at a family farm in Cheshire, studied surveying in Collinsville, and received hands-on training with the land, first on a Waterbury farm and then at his own farm in Guilford.

He thought parks were necessary for cities as both literal and figurative breaths of fresh air for all urban dwellers. Olmsted, sometimes with partners, designed Bridgeport's Seaside and Beardsley parks and Walnut Hill Park in New Britain. He also laid out the 35 acres of a Hartford mental health center, the Institute of Living, and consulted on the development of Trinity College's campus for more than 20

OLMSTED IN CONNECTICUT

What: Frederick Law Olmsted's Connecticut legacy

Where: Various

Cost: Free

Noteworthy: There's a bust of Frederick Law Olmsted near the entrance to the Institute of Living on Retreat Avenue in Hartford.

Olmsted was a *New York Times* reporter, and during the Civil War he oversaw the private United States Sanitary Commission, which supported the medical corps in treating wounded Union soldiers.

Walnut Hill Park in New Britain is among the Connecticut parks and other landscapes designed by Frederick Law Olmsted, best known for Manhattan's Central Park. Photo courtesy of Wikipedia.

years. The 11 known Connecticut residential commissions he or his firm planned include Branford's Pine Orchard and the family housing for Groton's US Navy Submarine Base.

Olmsted died in 1903 and is interred in the family vault at Hartford's Old North Cemetery.

His son and stepson continued his landscape architecture firm, and the legacy of Olmsted-created green spaces has continued in Connecticut with projects including Waveny Park in New Canaan and Hubbard Park in Meriden.

ACTION WILDLIFE (page 112)
Photo by Anastasia Mills Healy

THIMBLE ISLANDS (page 32)
Photo by Anastasia Mills Healy

BARKHAMSTED LIGHTHOUSE (page 43)
Photo courtesy Coni Dubois

LOUIS' LUNCH (page 184)
Photo by Steve Healy

HOGPEN HILL FARMS (page 22)
Photo by Anastasia Mills Healy

CUSHING CENTER (page 40)
Photo courtesy of Terry Dagradi, Yale University

GLASS HOUSE (page 164)
Photo by Anastasia Mills Healy

BRIDGEWATER (page 130)
Photo by Anastasia Mills Healy

BOOM BOX PARADE (page 58)
Photo courtesy of Eleanor Linkkila

DINOSAUR PLACE (page 176)
Photo by Anastasia Mills Healy

NORTHWAY (page 110)
Photo courtesy of ChiChi Ubiña

HILL-STEAD (page 142)
Photo courtesy of Hill-Stead

FISH CHURCH (page 50)
Photo courtesy of Robert Gregson

Arethusa Farm
Litchfield, CT

ARETHUSA (page 26)
Photo courtesy of Arethusa Farm Dairy

MERRITT PARKWAY (page 150)
Photo courtesy of Library of Congress

A WOODSTOCK NAKATION

What's so special about this resort?

In the northeastern part of the state near the Massachusetts border, a gravel road leads to a 360-acre, member-owned resort, where generations of families have been spending summers since 1934.

There's a real sense of community, with friendly members competing in shuffleboard tournaments, boogying at poolside DJ parties, and participating in scavenger hunts. Sunshine Stretch is a popular morning activity, and the lake's private beach is a serene spot to relax. Kids run around the playground, play ping-pong in the game room, paddle canoes, and make art and crafts in the pavilion.

Sounds nice, but why is Solair Recreation League in this book? It's a nudist resort. Begone, uptight Puritan New England Connecticut Yankee stereotype!

This family-friendly retreat, where hundreds of people who enjoy nude recreation spend time in a bucolic, private setting, is not a swinging singles commune. Affiliated with the American Association for Nude Recreation (AANR, founded in 1931), Solair runs background checks on proposed members and requires four visits and approval from the membership director before joining. No photography is allowed.

Because the resort is so large, many of its 350 members and associates zip around from the Olympic-size pool to the hiking trailheads and from the Sunday Sundae socials to the tennis

Founded in 1934, Solair Recreation League is a 360-acre, members-only family naturist resort. Photo courtesy of Solair Recreation League.

courts in golf carts. There's even a cafe, so you don't need to leave when lunchtime rolls around.

Accommodations are a mix of small cabins and RV and tent sites. There are more than 50 rental properties and triple that number of member sites, some which are available to rent.

Solair's season is April 15 through October 31, so pack your bathing suit—oh, wait, no, don't.

AANR reports serving 52 million people at 200 affiliated clubs, resorts, RV campgrounds, and businesses.

AMERICA'S FIRST SPA RESORT

Could Stafford Springs have ended up like Saratoga?

Stafford Springs didn't need pharmaceutical reps—doctors themselves touted the curative properties of its mineral water. The Nipmuck people told the white settlers about the springs' health benefits, and it didn't take long for word to spread through doctors, newspaper accounts, and word of mouth.

An intriguing figure, Dr. Joseph Warren, was physician to many statesmen, including John Adams. Warren bought property in Stafford Springs, where he planned to build a sanitorium. To generate interest, he wrote a 1766 article in the *Boston Gazette*. Stafford became a stage coach stop 1767, and people with ailments including "scrophulous humours," "lax fibre," and rheumatism set their hopes on the iron- and sulphur-rich water.

Adams was a hypochondriac, and Warren sent him on a spa vacation in June 1771. He was not issued a plush robe and slippers in a marble hydrotherapy room. Instead, Adams found a wooden shed built over a reservoir and was handed "a glass mug, broken to pieces and painted together again" to drink water he described as having yellow sediment and tasting like steel. The proprietors, the Childses, charged eight pennies. He wrote in his diary, "Thirty people have been to the spring today—the halt, the lame, the hypochondriac, the scrofulous, etc."

Dr. Joseph Warren was a patriot who sent Paul Revere on his ride, wrote the anthem, "Free America," and might have spied on the British.

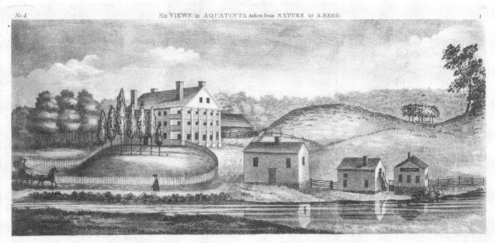

The healing powers of the mineral-rich waters of Stafford Springs drew early spa goers including John Adams, who kept a diary of his visit. Photo courtesy of Library of Congress.

Dr. Warren did not get to build his resort—he died at Bunker Hill in 1775. Another physician, Dr. Samuel Willard, took up the charge and erected the Springs House Hotel, which welcomed guests in greater style than the Childses for many years. It closed in 1896 and, since then, those with scrophulous humours have had to go to Saratoga.

HEALING WATERS

What: America's first spa resort

Where: Stafford Springs

Cost: N/A

Noteworthy: The Stafford Historic District is on the National Register of Historic Places.

SHADE SWAMP SANCTUARY

Why are there large cages in a Farmington swamp?

If a hiker stumbled upon large cages in the woods, alarm would be an understandable reaction. But there's no need to panic about the nearly two dozen abandoned enclosures at Farmington's Shade Swamp Sanctuary.

The cages sit within 800 acres of state-owned wetlands and woods on a blue-blazed hiking trail, just off busy Route 6. Pheasants, owls, and raccoons were among the animals that lived in these wire-fenced pens; some also have little stone huts. The state founded the site in 1926 as a sanctuary for wildlife that was native to the state, and scientists also used it to study and breed animals and birds, like starlings. The property was open to the public, and a summer Sunday could bring as many as 3,000 visitors.

In 1934, Civilian Conservation Corps workers from Camp Roberts in Thomaston built the cages and a wooden shelter, which is now on the National Register of Historic Places, at the beginning of the blue trail. But after losing funding, the caretaker was let go and the caged animals were transferred to other sites. The area still was considered a sanctuary for native species (not like the monkeys, alligator, and giraffe people tried giving them). Through the 1960s, the town promoted the trails and groups gathered for events. The site officially closed in 1983, but the Farmington Garden Club maintains it.

New England's first female nature guide, Mary Pasco, educated Shade Swamp Sanctuary visitors about the site's flora and fauna in the summer of 1934.

The woods of the Shade Swamp Sanctuary hold the remains of a state-run wildlife sanctuary and scientific research station. Photo courtesy of National Archives.

Photo courtesy of Connecticut Historical Commission.

There's a small parking area and two marked trails that people have found (as evidenced by vandalism). The animals that were initially intended to live in the cages are long gone, but some creatures of the forest and swamp seem to be happy to have shelter.

WHAT WENT ON IN THESE WOODS?

What: Hiking trail past an abandoned zoo

Where: Rte. 6 just west of Rte. 10 intersection, Farmington

Cost: Free

Pro Tip: Wear bug spray and check for ticks.

LET THEM EAT GREY POUPON

Why is this house fit for royalty?

One expects a Rolls-Royce to pull up at any moment with an English gentleman inquiring, "Pardon me, would you have any Grey Poupon?" as in the famous commercial.

One of the wealthiest communities in the United States, Greenwich certainly has its fair share of stunning homes. There are quite a few on North Street, but none as special as the stately white mansion at the end of an impressive double row of trees. Often mistaken for a replica of the White House, this Neoclassical stunner is instead a very close facsimile of the Petit Trianon of Versailles. The only reason it's not a complete doppelgänger is that, as a condition to be able to build this beauty, the French government stipulated something had to be changed, so the main staircase was built in the opposite direction. Petit Trianon Deux also reflects other design variations, but maintains the perfect proportions of the original.

The last queen of France, Marie Antoinette, most famously used the original Petit Trianon as a private retreat. A Chicago heir to the Goodrich Tire fortune, Laura Robinson, built the Greenwich one, called Northway, in 1911.

Northway's American architects, J. Edwin Carpenter and Walter D. Blair, both attended the Ecole des Beaux Arts in Paris and purposefully created the illusion that Northway was erected

Robinson married Goodrich Tire executive William Evans in 1915. Both he and their son died within months of each other in 1939.

Sometimes mistaken for a replica of the White House, this private Neoclassical home was modeled on Marie Antoinette's Versailles palace, the Petit Trianon. Photo courtesy of Chichi Ubiña.

NORTHWAY

What: A bit of France in Greenwich

Where: Private home on North St., Greenwich

Cost: N/A

Pro Tip: This is a private, gated home on a busy street. To get a look inside, watch the 2004 Val Kilmer and Carrie Fisher movie *Stateside*, which was directed by the owner.

in the 18th century. The facade of the home, on 12 acres reached by a formal allée, features four grand Corinthian columns and a rooftop baluster with an urn design. Past the rectangular reflecting pool with fountains, a divided staircase leads to a raised entry court and tall French doors. Inside, a pipe organ sits under 15-foot ceilings at the foot of a divided marble staircase. Isn't that where your organ is?

A SAFARI IN LITCHFIELD

Did you know that you can go on safari in Goshen?

Northwestern Connecticut is not the first place on adventurers' lists when they plan a safari. Yet, in Goshen, there's an 18-acre safari trail where cars can loop around big pens and pull over to get close-up looks at American bison, African Watusi cattle, and three zebras.

There are plenty of other animals at Action Wildlife Foundation without the exotic cachet, like pigs, goats, and sheep. In pre-COVID-19 times, you could stop by the petting zoo to feed animals with a baby bottle or hand-feed them pellets.

It's a large property—116 acres—that's challenging to protect from coyotes. Even with fences, owner Jim Mazzarelli has killed as many as 100 coyotes in a year. This hasn't prevented these predators from picking off Action Wildlife's animals, though; recent losses include a water buffalo and emu. He's working on filling the empty pens and is considering South American capybara and peacocks.

Coyotes aren't the only animals Mazzarelli has killed. Action Wildlife also has a natural history museum with taxidermied creatures including a rhinoceros and a grizzly bear, all of which Mazzarelli hunted personally. The animals are in realistic poses—one bison head butts another, an elk fights a bear, a leopard hisses at a hyena from a tree. There's a water buffalo here to make up for the missing one in the safari park, and a separate room displays animals endemic to Connecticut like black bear, red fox, and turkey.

SELF-DRIVE SAFARI

What: Safari experience and museum

Where: 337 Torrington Rd., Goshen

Cost: $5 per person

Pro Tip: The animal population increases drastically in spring, which brings approximately 85 babies.

112

Zebras and Watusi cattle are some of the animals that can be spotted on a self-drive safari; more exotic, taxidermied creatures are on display in the on-site museum. Photos courtesy of Anastasia Mills Healy.

Mazzarelli, a senior citizen with more energy than many people half his age, has been running this safari-zoo-museum hybrid for about two decades and shows no signs of stopping. Break out your camo and binoculars and head to Connecticut's safari park!

One of the animals in the museum is a snow leopard, which is endangered, but don't call the Department of Fish & Wildlife. It's actually a mountain lion in disguise.

A FEW GOOD MEN

What role did New London play in the Amistad affair?

A critical event in the struggle toward abolishing slavery in the United States played out mainly in Connecticut. Of the state's numerous locations connected to the Amistad affair, the US Custom House (now a maritime museum) is perhaps the least known, as is the critical role of New London resident Dwight Janes.

In 1839, when African Mende captives revolted and commandeered the Cuban ship *La Amistad*, the ship's crew capitalized on the Africans' lack of navigation knowledge and sailed north to America instead of east to Africa. Off Montauk Point, the US Navy brig USS *Washington* seized the ship in New York and escorted it to New London.

An active abolitionist, Janes was an observer aboard the USS *Washington* during the initial legal inquiry. He ascertained that the Mende were freeborn Africans, not Cuban slaves as the Spanish owners claimed. This distinction was critical, as was Janes's subsequent trial testimonies and his dogged efforts to recruit men who would represent the Amistad captives.

Janes was a New London grocer, not a lawyer. He wrote three letters apiece to abolitionists Roger Baldwin, Joshua Leavitt, and Lewis Tappan, all of whom ended up working on the Mendes' legal defense as part of the Amistad Committee. After numerous trials that ended with the Supreme Court freeing them, in 1842, the survivors arrived in Sierra Leone.

Other Connecticut Amistad-related sites include: The New Haven Museum & Historical Society, New Haven's Amistad Memorial, and the Farmington Historical Society; see ctfreedomtrail.org/trail/amistad/sites.

New London's Custom House Maritime Museum explains the city's pivotal role in the Amistad affair. Photo courtesy of New London Maritime Society.

Meanwhile, *La Amistad* remained moored at New London's Lawrence Pier until after the trials, when the city's US Custom inspector auctioned off the ship and its cargo.

One in ten slave ships had revolts, but their stories didn't end with freedom. "The only thing necessary for the triumph of evil is for good men to do nothing."

AMISTAD INFO

What: New London's role in the Amistad affair told in a rare exhibit

Where: Custom House Maritime Museum, 150 Bank St., New London

Cost: Free–$7

Noteworthy: The nation's oldest continuously operating US Custom House was designed by architect Robert Mills, best known for the Washington Monument.

EDUCATION PIONEERS

Who is the girl in the sculpture and what education reform did she inspire?

A girl stands in cupped hands at the busy Hartford intersection of Cogswell Street, Asylum Avenue, and Farmington Avenue. She is Alice Cogswell, the child who inspired the founding of America's first permanent school for the deaf and first school in the country for people with any disability.

In 1807, the two-year-old daughter of Hartford physician Dr. Mason Fitch Cogswell had an illness that resulted in hearing loss. The doctor spearheaded a survey to discover the extent of deafness in the community and, finding 84 deaf people in Connecticut, extrapolated that there would be enough students for a school. At that point, deaf children did not receive an education and were not thought of as intellectually equal to the hearing.

Cogswell raised enough money in one afternoon to send Thomas Gallaudet to Europe to learn proven methods of teaching deaf students. Gallaudet brought a deaf French teacher, Laurent Clerc, back to Hartford; on the 55-day journey, Clerc taught Gallaudet sign language and Gallaudet taught Clerc English. Together with Dr. Cogswell, they opened the Connecticut Asylum at Hartford for the Instruction of Deaf and Dumb Persons in 1817. Now called the American School for the Deaf, it has educated 4,000 people, who have gone on to teach many others.

Daniel Chester French created a sculpture of Thomas Gallaudet and Alice Cogswell for Gallaudet University in 1888 that was recast in 1924 for the American School for the Deaf.

At age two, Alice Cogswell lost her hearing, prompting her physician father to help found what became the American School for the Deaf. Photo courtesy of Wikimedia Commons.

AMERICAN SCHOOL FOR THE DEAF

What: Pioneering special education

Where: American School for the Deaf, 139 North Main St., West Hartford

Cost: Various

Noteworthy: Thomas Gallaudet was a direct descendant of Thomas Hooker, the founder of Connecticut and pastor of Hartford's Center Church.

Gallaudet's son became the founding president of what is now Gallaudet University in Washington, DC; it remains the only liberal arts college in the world for the deaf.

The giant hands that hold Alice make the sign for "light," referencing the opportunities that Gallaudet helped bring to deaf people through education.

117

SERGEANT STUBBY

What did this dog do to become a celebrity?

He served with distinction in France during World War I, captured an enemy spy, met three presidents, and personally was awarded a medal by General John Pershing. His name was Stubby, and he was a dog.

A friendly brindle puppy with a short tail wandered into a training camp near the Yale Bowl in October 1917. The soldiers of the 102nd Infantry, 26th Yankee Division, were so taken by Stubby that Private J. Robert Conroy smuggled him aboard the SS *Minnesota* in an overcoat. His commanding officer discovered him, but after Stubby saluted he was allowed to stay.

Stubby warned the 102nd about gas attacks, found wounded soldiers on the battlefield, and was wounded himself. In the Argonne, Stubby spotted a German soldier doing reconnaissance on the Allied trenches. The soldier tried to befriend him, but Stubby growled, attacked, and pinned him. For capturing an enemy spy, Stubby was promoted to sergeant, becoming the first dog in the United

CANINE WAR HERO

What: Canine celebrity war hero

Where: West Haven Veterans Museum and Learning Center, 30 Hood Terr., West Haven

Cost: Free

Noteworthy: Stubby can be seen at the Smithsonian in Washington, DC, in the *Price of Freedom* exhibit at the National Museum of American History.

The West Haven Veterans Museum and Learning Center has a 1926 portrait of Sergeant Stubby by Charles Ayer Whipple and a diorama of World War I trenches, featuring tiny hidden replicas of him.

A stray who saluted, identified mustard gas, and captured a German soldier, Sergeant Stubby served with honor in 17 battles. Photos courtesy of West Haven Veterans Museum and Learning Center.

States Armed Forces to be given rank. By the time he returned home, Stubby had served in 17 battles.

Stubby's story swept the nation. He led parades and met presidents Wilson, Harding, and Coolidge. None other than General John Pershing, the Commanding General of the United States Armies, presented him with a medal in 1921.

Then, Stubby went to college, becoming the mascot of the Georgetown Hoyas football team when Conroy attended law school. When this canine hero died in 1926, his *New York Times* obituary was half a page long and three columns wide. This stray dog from New Haven had saved lives and captured the heart of a nation.

BEFORE HER TIME

Did you know that Connecticut has a State Heroine?

Maria Davis, the free Black housekeeper at Prudence Crandall's Canterbury Female Boarding School, sat in on classes, as did her soon-to-be sister-in-law, Sarah Harris. Harris wanted to teach Black children, so she became a day student in 1832. Crandall put her Quaker belief in the equality of all people to the test, and many parents of her white students pulled their daughters from the school.

But she didn't capitulate and teach only white girls. Instead, she made the radical decision to teach only Black girls.

In another unorthodox move, she traveled alone to Boston to meet with the publisher of the *Liberator* newspaper. So Crandall could recruit their daughters, William Lloyd Garrison provided letters of introduction to Black preachers and others in nearby states who belonged to the small Black community that could afford the $25 per quarter tuition. On April 1, 1833, Crandall started classes, and eventually approximately 20 brave "Young Ladies and Little Misses of Colour" came from states including New York, Rhode Island, and Pennsylvania.

Townspeople threatened fines and whipping, harassed students, polluted their well, refused to sell them food, broke a window with a rock, and set the school on fire. A new Black Law that made it illegal for Black people to cross state lines for education resulted in three court cases against Crandall and a night in jail. On September 9, 1834, vigilante violence erupted again, and she closed the school.

In 1886, the state awarded Crandall a $400 pension and Mark Twain offered to buy back her former school, but she was 83 and living in Kansas.

A pioneer in the fight for equal access to education, Prudence Crandall faced much opposition head on when she opened a school for Black girls in 1833. Photo courtesy of Prudence Crandall Museum.

Crandall lived to see the eradication of the Black Law and the passage of the 13th and 14th amendments, but it wasn't until 1954 that all people in the US were granted the right to an unsegregated education.

PRUDENCE CRANDALL MUSEUM

What: A pioneer in equal access to education

Where: 1 S. Canterbury Rd., Canterbury

Cost: Undetermined at press time

Noteworthy: Prudence Crandall is Connecticut's State Heroine. The museum is located in her former school in Canterbury, and there's a statue of her in the State Capitol.

MOVING MOUNTAINS

Why is there a giant, glowing cross above Waterbury?

Visible from Interstate 84, a 50-foot cross on a 10-foot pedestal rises high above Waterbury, glowing and changing colors.

A Catholic lawyer who had once attended seminary, Waterbury native John Greco, began creating what he called a religious theme park in the mid-1950s on Pine Hill. It didn't have a rollercoaster or Ferris wheel like a typical theme park; instead, Holy Land USA brought the Bible to life by recreating religious scenes, buildings, and displays. At its peak, 40,000 visitors a year were drawn to the middle of Waterbury to stroll through Jerusalem and Bethlehem to see depictions of saints, Jesus's manger, and the Temple of Herod. The faithful came to reflect on God in a chapel and by moving through the 14 Stations of the Cross.

With his health failing, Greco closed Holy Land USA in 1984 and sold it to an order of nuns in New Jersey. He died in 1986, and the park fell victim to the elements and to vandalism. Enter Waterbury residents and best friends Neil O'Leary and Fritz Blasius, who created a nonprofit to manage the 18-acre site and

HOLY LAND USA

What: A religious-themed park undergoing renewal

Where: 60 Slocum St., Waterbury

Cost: Free to drive past

Noteworthy: Except for special occasions, Holy Land is not yet open to the public.

Waterbury native Father Michael McGivney, founder of the Knights of Columbus, was beatified in 2020; a statue of him stands at Grand and Meadow streets.

A 50-foot cross that changes color according to the liturgical calendar marks the location of Holy Land USA. Photo courtesy of Wikipedia.

raise funds for its renewal. Since they became involved in 2013, the site has hosted events including dinners, Mountaintop Masses, and a Blessing of the Bikes (motorcycles). The nonprofit has erected a new cross with LED lights, and it changes colors according to the liturgical calendar.

There are repaved driveways at Holy Land USA, a refreshed website, and a Facebook page with 19,000 likes. The site shows indications of being on its way to renewal as a peaceful spiritual mountaintop haven for the community to gather, once again.

WHOA, NELLIE!

What do you know about the horseback riders in parades?

Not many people can get up in the morning, mount a horse, and go to work at a job that's remained remarkably consistent since the 18th century.

Meet the First Company Governor's Horse Guards (1CoGHG), founded in Hartford in 1778 by Revolutionary War veterans. Their first deployment was greeting newly elected President George Washington on October 19, 1789 when he visited Hartford; 1CoGHG has been a part of countless parades and ceremonial occasions ever since.

They also are trained in emergency operations and traffic and crowd control, and they can be called to active service to augment the Connecticut National Guard. The troop is part of the Connecticut Militia, along with the Army National Guard, the Air National Guard, a second horse guard troop, and two units of foot guards.

1CoGHG officers fought in the War of 1812, protected US interests against Pancho Villa in 1916, and served in France during World War I as part of the 101st Machine Gun Battalion.

HORSE GUARDS

What: The nation's oldest continuously active mounted cavalry unit

Where: 280 Arch Rd., Avon

Cost: Free

Pro Tip: The troop's drills are open to the public every Thursday, beginning at 7 p.m.

No military or equestrian experience is necessary to join this historic, all-volunteer troop that relies largely on private donations.

The first assignment for the First Company Governor's Horse Guards was greeting President George Washington on a 1789 Hartford visit; the unit has been active ever since. Photo courtesy of Deb Key Imagery.

In World War II, they manned anti-aircraft artillery on American soil, and many members deployed in the South Pacific.

The troop cares for and trains with 10 donated horses in Avon; their barn dates to 1880. Every summer, they do field training that includes weaponry, marches, and mounted and dismounted close-order drills. They also go on an overnight bivouac with the horses, using the same camping and horse-tying methods used by the troop for more than two centuries.

ADRIAEN WHO?

Who was the European who explored Connecticut before the Mayflower arrived?

We could all be speaking Dutch. The first European to sail up the Connecticut River was a man who is barely mentioned in history texts, but his discoveries charted what would become Connecticut and led to a Dutch settlement in what now is Hartford.

From Amsterdam, Adriaen Courtsen Block (c. 1567–1627) was a world explorer who traveled to the New World several times. In 1614, he sailed into the Long Island Sound to the Connecticut River, which he called *de Versche Rivier* (the Fresh River). A map he drew was the first to outline many elements of the mid-Atlantic and to use the label "New Netherland."

His reports set the stage for a 1633 Dutch fort called *Huys de Hoop* (House of Hope) at the mouth of the Park River near what now is Hartford. It was a busy trading post where the Dutch engaged Native Americans to hunt for beaver to fuel the European beaver-hat craze. By 1650, the Dutch were sending 80,000 pelts a year to Europe, and the beaver population became decimated.

New England colonists relied on the Dutch for many goods in the mid-17th century as the English Civil War restricted trade; Massachusetts even used Dutch currency. House of Hope was intended to be the capital of Dutch Connecticut but, as more and more colonists came south in response to Puritan austerity,

---

SAILING DUTCHMAN

What: Little-known Dutch adventurer credited with first exploring Connecticut

Where: Connecticut

Cost: N/A

Noteworthy: Hartford has a Huyshope Avenue and a mixed-use economic development project called Adriaen's Landing.

THE FIRST DUTCH SETTLEMENT, ADRIAEN BLOCK, 1614

Adriaen Block sailed up the Connecticut River in 1614 and his reports resulted in the Dutch trading center Huys de Hoop in what is now Hartford; the Dutch were instrumental in the early settlement of New England, but they gave up rights to Connecticut in 1667. Photo courtesy of Library of Congress.

the English outnumbered the Dutch. The two countries agreed on a border 50 miles west of the Connecticut River in 1650, but the Dutch gave up Connecticut completely in 1667 in exchange for the Indonesian spice trade (which included nutmeg).

Block named Block Island after himself and is credited with calling Rhode Island "Roode Eylandt" because of the red ("rood") soil he saw.

MADAME BUTTERFLY ON THE MIANUS

Why are these Victorian-era artists wearing kimonos?

In 1897, the sight of mixed male and female company kneeling on a porch in a quiet Connecticut neighborhood would have raised eyebrows. Add the fact that they were wearing kimonos and holding parasols, and you'd have had a real head-turner.

Following the 1854 opening of Japan to the West, Japanism—the influence of Japanese art and culture on Western fine and decorative arts—was pervasive first in Europe and later in America. At the height of Japanism in the US, Japanese art student Genjiro Yeto enrolled in classes at the Art Students League in Manhattan. One of his instructors, John Henry Twachtman, invited him to paint *en plein air* at an artists' retreat in the waterfront village of Cos Cob. Twachtman was a Greenwich resident who spent time at the Holley boarding house, which had been accessible to New Yorkers by train since 1848. This bucolic spot on the Mianus River became the state's first American Impressionist art colony. It's open to the public today as the National Historic Landmark Bush-Holley House, under the stewardship of the Greenwich Historical Society.

Yeto first came to the Holley House in 1895 and spent part of each year there until 1901. He was friendly with fellow artist Elmer Livingston MacRae, who married the daughter of the

GENJIRO YETO

What: Japanism at Connecticut's first American Impressionist art colony

Where: 47 Strickland Rd., Cos Cob

Cost: Free–$10

Pro Tip: The Greenwich Historical Society can arrange a Japanese-language tour and has information available in Japanese.

Genjiro Yeto taught members of the Cos Cob American Impressionist art colony about Japanese art and culture. Photo courtesy of Greenwich Historical Society.

boarding house proprietors in 1900. Under Yeto's tutelage, Constant Holley MacRae became accomplished in the art of ikebana flower arranging. The artists got caught up in Japanism, making origami, holding tea ceremonies, and dressing in kimonos.

Yeto achieved success as a watercolorist and illustrator and was a cultural consultant for the original Broadway production of *Madame Butterfly*, which inspired Puccini's opera along with the earlier short story on which they both were based.

Yeto's artwork often is on display in the Greenwich Historical Society's Permanent Collection Gallery.

FIRSTS AND LASTS IN BRIDGEWATER

Why can you now order a chardonnay at The Village Bistro?

There's one traffic light in the bucolic, 16-square-mile town of Bridgewater, which was the last town in Connecticut to sell liquor (2015) and the first to operate a nationwide mail-order business (1866).

The town has records from the early 1700s of selling hard cider and cider brandy called "winkum"—so named as "it seemed to first affect the eyes, before the state of being tipsy occurred." There were two taverns in town in the 1800s, but when an inn asked to sell wine in the mid-1900s, the request was denied. The 1,700 Bridgewater residents, mostly middle-age and older, wanted to keep the small-town vibe intact.

Finally, in 2015, the town voted to allow liquor sales, and its quaintness has not been damaged. A recent visit uncovered a charming 1899 complex with an upscale convenience store and sophisticated casual restaurant (which serves alcohol) next to a post office.

Charles Thompson was 14 when he began selling low-cost trinkets and toys in 1866 from a nearby building. Later, from his office on the third floor of this 50-foot, Queen Anne tower, the flamboyant "Mail Order King" oversaw upwards of 1,000 daily orders. They stemmed from his nationwide reach of ads and salesmen hawking soap and perfume, like his most popular

At the Shepaug Valley School, kids from Bridgewater can study agriscience, gaining experience with hydroponics, drones, and biofuel development.

Charles Thompson ran a successful mail-order business beginning in 1866, and The Village Bistro has been open and able to serve liquor since 2016. Photo by Anastasia Mills Healy.

brand, Perfumo, "before postal laws brought an end to his empire," according to the National Register of Historic Places.

Let's see a show of hands for The Village Bistro and The Village Store bringing back respectively winkum and Perfumo.

BRIDGEWATER

What: Connecticut's last dry town and first national mail-order business

Where: 27 Main Street S., Bridgewater

Cost: Various

Pro Tip: The Village Bistro's "Big Pancake" is no joke.

A CAMP FOR ADULTS

Why are 30-year-olds playing capture the flag?

Campers go canoeing on a private lake, tie-dye T-shirts, take counselor-led hikes, make s'mores around a campfire, and sleep in cabins. What's so special about that? The campers are adults.

There's basically every activity imaginable available on Club Getaway's 310 acres, from ziplining to tennis and archery to mountain biking. Unusual camp activities: morning wake-up raves, Bloody Mary bingo, paint and sip class, and pub hikes (walking from keg to keg). Ziplining at 36 mph and plummeting 40 feet on the Geronimo Jump's bungee are not for the faint of heart. Happy hours, karaoke, and races on enormous paddleboards that can fit 10 people also are part of the adult fun.

That's not to say that kids never run rampant deliriously from activity to activity. Children definitely are welcome at certain times, but groups don't intermingle. There are family camps, Gen X camps, LGBTQ+ weekends, a Gilmore Girls fan weekend, and even a weekend themed around the actor John Waters (who wants to bet there are pink flamingos involved?).

At Club Getaway, counselors are "social coordinators" and COVID-19 changes include socially distanced concerts and cabins shared only by pre-organized small groups. Good to note: Cabins are air-conditioned and heated, and the beds have 10-inch memory foam mattresses.

CAMPING IN KENT

What: Camp for adults

Where: 59 S. Kent Rd., Kent

Cost: Varies, starting at about $475 per weekend.

Pro Tip: Club Getaway is all about themes, so check the website to make sure you're booking the right weekend for your interests.

Adults can enjoy the usual fun camp activities in addition to adult-oriented events like wake-up raves and pub hikes. Photos courtesy of Eric Nurbin.

Not that you need any more activities, but there are great design stores, art galleries, cafes, and an excellent bookstore in downtown Kent. The waterfall, which can be seen from the parking lot at Kent Falls State Park, definitely is worth a visit as well.

Check out the Bravo reality show filmed at Club Getaway, *Camp Getaway*.

REUNITING EUROPE IN MIDDLEFIELD

What is a jostaberry?

"The story's bigger than the production," says John Lyman, whose Lyman Orchards produces between 600 and 1,000 pounds of jostaberries a year.

Pronounced YA-sta-ber-ry, this cross between a black currant and a gooseberry is uncommon in America. "You don't run across it at all," he says. So, why for two weeks in July can you pick jostaberries in Connecticut?

In the 1980s, Lyman learned that "a West German plant breeder came up with a plan to reunite Europe" by crossing two berries that were popular in different European countries. First made available to the public in 1977, they were a novelty, and Lyman was intrigued. He first planted them in 1988 and he hasn't looked back. They took several years to grow and start producing fruit, but when they did, people were curious and jostaberries caught on. "They have a very loyal following," he says. He explained that the grocer Big Y wanted to buy some of his production, but that his own customers consumed the crop in full.

Jostaberries have health benefits, with high levels of antioxidants and vitamin C. They're tart, so sugar is usually part of recipes; Lyman Orchards sells a jam using a recipe they developed. Lyman says that people also make syrup and baste meat with them.

In the late 18th and early 19th centuries, America and England went so crazy over gooseberries that there were gooseberry appreciation clubs.

Lyman Orchards has found a following for its annual crop of jostaberries, which are rare in the US. Photo courtesy of Lyman Orchards.

Connecticut farmers grow some unusual food including poona kheera cucumbers, figs, and lemongrass. Eat your way around the state and unite the world.

JOSTABERRIES

What: Jostaberries

Where: 105 South St., Middlefield

Cost: Various

Pro Tip: Try Lyman Orchards' tri-berry muffins made with jostaberries, blueberries, and raspberries.

CALLING ALL SCHOLARS AND SPACE NUTS

How do you encompass the human imagination in one room?

Not everyone would be able to concentrate when surrounded by an original 1957 Russian Sputnik, "Thing" from *The Addams Family*, and a 300-million-year-old trilobite fossil. There are tens of thousands of items in Jay Walker's library; most are books, but many are rare and/or obscure items drawn from science.

Other space-themed items include models of the Saturn V rocket and X-29 jet, a meteorite, the autographs of nine astronauts who walked on the moon, and an EKG showing Buzz Aldrin's even heart rate on a death-defying descent.

As for rare books, there are hand-painted coronation albums, a page from an original Gutenberg Bible, and an atlas from 1699 reflecting for the first time the radical idea that the sun was the center of the solar system.

It's called the Walker Library of the History of Human Imagination, and Jay Walker knows a thing or two about the subject. He's a prolific inventor, with more than 450 patents either issued or pending. One of *Time*'s "50 most influential business leaders in the digital age," Walker is best known as the founder of Priceline.com but also is involved in many other pursuits.

The pursuit of freedom must hit home for him, since he owns one of two known copies of the Declaration of Independence made via the anastatic method, a kind of

---

A soaring three-story space with etched-glass panels that illuminate in sync with music, the 3,600-square-foot library building itself is inspirational.

One of two known anastatic copies of the Declaration of Independence and a handprinted Kelmscott Press edition of the Works of Geoffrey Chaucer are two of the Walker Library's many notable items. Photo on left courtesy of Library of Congress. Photo on right courtesy of the British Library.

early photocopy that probably contributed to the fading of the original. If any scholar, space nut, or Bond fan wants to see the copy, the chandelier from *Die Another Day*, or a Kelmscott edition of Chaucer, she'll have to wangle an invitation—the library isn't open to the public.

WALKER LIBRARY

What: Spectacular private library

Where: Private home in Ridgefield

Cost: N/A

Noteworthy: Access to the library is by invitation only; it's not open to the public.

"LONE EAGLE" IN CONNECTICUT

Did you know that the world's most famous aviator lived and worked in Connecticut?

If I were in the business of building airplanes, I'd try to get the world's most famous aviator to work for me. East Hartford's Pratt & Whitney, formerly a unit of United Aircraft (UA), did just that. When Charles Lindbergh touched down back in the United States after piloting the first nonstop transatlantic flight from New York to Paris in 1927, Hartford was his first stop. He landed at Brainard Field, rode in a parade, studied engines at the Pratt & Whitney factory, and began an American tour.

After working in commercial aviation and taking time to live quietly in England following the kidnapping and murder of his son, in 1943 Lindbergh joined UA in Connecticut and Ford in Michigan. His research and development efforts focused on testing B-24 Liberator bombers that were powered by Ford-produced Pratt & Whitney engines.

Lindbergh served on UA's engineering advisory committee and worked for the Chance Vought division in Stratford, where he participated in engineering conferences, flew F4U Corsair fighters on test flights, and advised on fighter plane design.

In the six months he spent in the Pacific during World War II representing UA, he flew 50 combat missions. Studying how

Aircraft designer Igor Sikorsky accompanied Lindbergh when he opened a Caribbean route for Pan Am in 1931, flying a Sikorsky S-40 amphibian powered by four Pratt & Whitney Hornet engines.

The first man to fly a solo, nonstop, transatlantic flight, Charles Lindbergh worked for Pratt & Whitney/United Aircraft and is pictured here with the company's WASP engine. Photo courtesy of Pratt & Whitney.

planes performed in combat conditions, he flew Corsairs in combat and took to the skies for air raids and special bombing missions.

Lindbergh returned to Connecticut, reported on the performance of the fighter planes, and after the war continued as a UA consultant. The Lindberghs kept a cottage in Darien for many years; Charles docked his seaplane in Scotts Cove when he lived on Tokeneke Trail.

CHARLES LINDBERGH

What: Charles Lindbergh's work in Connecticut

Where: Pratt & Whitney Hangar Museum, 423 Airport Ave., East Hartford

Cost: Free

Pro Tip: Items related to Lindbergh at Pratt & Whitney's museum (open Tues. and Thurs., 10 a.m.–3 p.m.), include his desk and a portrait of him.

WHO YA GONNA CALL?

What Monroe residents were famous paranormal authorities?

The Amityville Horror, *The Conjuring*, *Annabelle*, and *The Haunting in Connecticut* are horror movies based on occurrences that the first couple of the paranormal, Connecticut residents Lorraine and Ed Warren, investigated. Now deceased, the Warrens were a perfect couple: she was a trance medium and he a demonologist. For many years, they ran a museum on their property in Monroe, filled with objects from cases they investigated. The most famous looked like a harmless Raggedy Ann doll.

Created by Norwalk cartoonist Johnny Gruelle, part of the Silvermine arts scene in Norwalk in the early 20th century, Raggedy Ann became a popular mass-produced doll. According to the Warrens, in 1971 the spirit of a young girl named Annabelle possessed a Raggedy Ann doll and caused all manner of mayhem until she was enclosed in a glass case. Recent (unfounded) reports of her escape caused a worldwide social media frenzy.

SPOOKY STUFF

What: Connecticut's real-life ghostbusters

Where: Various

Cost: Free

Noteworthy: The Warrens investigated more than 10,000 cases of paranormal activity across the United States and as far away as Japan.

Lorraine Warren was a Roman Catholic who claimed her faith protected her against evil spirits; she often worked with priests, who provided blessings and exorcisms.

A Raggedy Ann doll reportedly possessed by a spirit named Annabelle is seen in a glass case; her story was one of several the Warrens investigated that became major feature films.
Photo courtesy of Flickering Myth.

Photo courtesy of Mysterious World.

The Warrens didn't charge for their investigations; their income came from books, lectures, and fees for licensing their stories for movie and television productions.

Their son-in-law, Tony Spera, now runs the New England Society for Psychic Research (N.E.S.P.R.), founded in 1952 by Ed and Lorraine, so you know who to call if you encounter a demonic doll or giant, evil Pillsbury Doughboy.

MONETS ON THE MOUNTAIN

Why is there a world-renowned French Impressionist collection in a Farmington house?

There are many lovely Colonial Revival homes in Connecticut, but only at Hill-Stead can one admire two Monets, a Manet, and a Degas from the drawing room—and that's only the beginning of the extraordinary art collection at this expansive 1901 estate. Alfred Pope traveled frequently to France and collected most of the French Impressionist works during the artists' lifetimes, when the style was not widely well-received.

After completing her studies at Miss Porter's School in 1888, Theodate Pope didn't have formal architectural training when she convinced both her father and the architectural firm McKim, Mead & White that she would design a new family home on 250 acres up the hill from the school. She eventually became one of America's first female architects, responsible for the Westover School and Avon Old Farms School, and for rehabilitating Theodore Roosevelt's Gramercy Park birthplace.

Roosevelt visited Hill-Stead, as did Mary Cassatt and Henry James, who wrote in his 1907 book *The American Scene* that it was: "a great new house on a hilltop that overlooked the most composed of communities; a house apparently conceived—and with great felicity—on the lines of a magnified Mount Vernon."

Hill-Stead provides a rare opportunity to be surrounded by world-renowned art—as well as original Duncan Phyfe furniture

---

In 1915, knocked unconscious and in the water for many hours, Theodate Pope barely survived the sinking of the *Lusitania*.

One of the country's first female architects, Theodate Pope designed her home, Hill-Stead, which is filled with Impressionist masterpieces. Photos courtesy of Hill-Stead.

and Ming dynasty porcelain— while feeling like an invited guest at an elegant yet comfortable home. However, please resist the temptation to sit on the couch.

Without changing the building footprint, a new exhibition gallery, new media space, and education center will open in 2021.

HILL-STEAD

What: Not your typical house museum

Where: 35 Mountain Rd., Farmington

Cost: Free–$18

Pro Tip: Take time to enjoy Hill-Stead's grounds; now 152 acres, they include a Beatrix Farrand–designed sunken garden, walking trails that traverse woodlands and meadows, and a flock of resident sheep.

HIDDEN COMMENTARY

Why is there a turtle on the Lafayette statue?

Next time you're zipping around the traffic circle in front of the Capitol in Hartford, look in front of the left hind hoof of the horse in the statue. Keen eyes will spot a turtle.

As a thank-you for the Statue of Liberty, America gifted France a statue of the Marquis de Lafayette in 1907. A copy of this statue was dedicated in Hartford in 1932 to pay tribute to a man who aided the Continental Army greatly during the American Revolution.

Barely out of his teens, Lafayette arrived in America in 1777 to fight under George Washington. A bridge between the countries, he garnered French troops whose support helped make possible the successful Yorktown blockade that ended the war.

A turtle seems out of place in a battle depiction of a great general, mounted with sword raised. Its sculptor, Paul Wayne Bartlett, was born in New Haven, moved to Paris as a child, and was well-known for his depictions of animals. Turtle theories include that Bartlett was remarking on delayed payment or the time it took to erect the statue. He received the commission in 1899 and delivered a plaster model the next year. By the time he presented the bronze statue seven years later, the figure's wig, tricorn hat, and clothes had changed and the horse was almost stepping on a turtle. So it seems that the gifted bronze animal renderer left a commentary on his own glacial pace of finishing the commission.

LAFAYETTE STATUE

What: A statue with a statement

Where: Capitol Ave. between Lafayette St. and Washington St., Hartford

Cost: Free

Noteworthy: Bartlett also is responsible for *Apotheosis of Democracy*, a marble pediment on the US Capitol.

The New Haven-born sculptor of the Hartford statue of General Lafayette added a turtle, possibly to remark on how long it took him to deliver the final statue. Photo courtesy of Library of Congress.

The Paris statue stood in front of the Louvre until, displaced by the I. M. Pei–designed glass pyramid, it moved to a spot between the Grand Palais and the Seine. Lafayette is buried in Paris with soil from Bunker Hill—the "Hero of Two Worlds" at rest, with no turtles in sight.

The French statue was commissioned by the Daughters of the American Revolution and paid for by pennies and nickels collected from American schoolchildren.

RADIANCE CAPTURED

Where can you see Tiffany stained glass?

The man responsible for the little blue box, Charles Lewis Tiffany, was born in Killingly. His eldest son, Louis Comfort Tiffany, was a New York City resident, but he spent much time in Connecticut, and exquisite stained glass windows across the state attest to his skilled artistry.

Tiffany's sister had a home in New London, and both families spent time together there in the late 19th century. The city's St. James Episcopal Church glows with six Tiffany windows; two enchanting angels in the charming Pequot Chapel, which he frequented, are his work. There also are six Tiffany windows at Christ Church in Pomfret, and a five-window series in the Norfolk Congregational Church is of particular note for the magnificent depiction of the four seasons. There are no fewer than 18 Tiffany windows in Fairfield's First Church Congregational, and they also grace churches in Hartford, Meriden, Brooklyn, Norwich, Winsted, and Greenwich, among others.

Tiffany reached the highest level of craftsmanship in stained glass, but he worked in many media and had a design firm called Associated Artists that created interiors for the Chester Arthur White House and Mark Twain's Hartford home. Both he and Twain had been inspired by travels in North Africa, and the rooms on the first floor of Twain's house reflect this embrace of "Orientalism" with red-painted walls and detailed geometric

---

Mark Twain and Harriet Beecher Stowe lived right next to each other; both homes now are museums. Stowe's brother was a minister who performed the marriage of Twain and his wife.

Louis Comfort Tiffany spent time in Connecticut, and his spectacular stained glass windows can be found throughout the state; he also was an interior designer whose clients included Mark Twain. Photo courtesy of Library of Congress.

stenciling. There also was once a Tiffany window depicting lilies in the entry.

Tiffany was a talented painter and accomplished in enamelwork, metalwork, pottery, mosaic, and other media, but it's his ability to paint in glass and create windows that radiate the sublime found in God and nature for which he will be most remembered.

TIFFANY STAINED GLASS

What: Tiffany in Connecticut

Where: Various

Cost: Churches, free; Mark Twain House, free–$18; Harriet Beecher Stowe Center, free–$16

Noteworthy: Tiffany's innovations include creating shading and texture in molten glass in a patented technique he called favrile.

"I AM NO POLITICIAN"

Why did P. T. Barnum go into politics?

Cursory knowledge of P. T. Barnum often will include his relationship to Barnum & Bailey's Greatest Show on Earth and to a museum showcasing intriguing items. Tufts University grads know that Barnum was a founder and that their beloved mascot, Jumbo, was named for one of his elephants. Those who have seen *The Greatest Showman* are aware that Barnum's American Museum was destroyed by arsonists. What is not as well known is where Barnum was when he learned of the fire.

Barnum said, "I am no politician," yet he ran for the House of Representatives "simply because I wished to have the honor of voting for the two constitutional amendments—one for driving slavery entirely out of the country; the other to allow men of education and good moral character to vote, regardless of the color of their skins." He was elected in the pivotal year of 1865, served three other terms, and also was mayor of Bridgeport in 1875.

"All men are equally children of the common Father," he said in support of granting Black men the right to vote. "Let no man attach an eternal stigma to his name by shutting his eyes to the great lesson of the hour."

On July 13, 1865, a telegram with the news that his museum was hopelessly in flames interrupted a speech Barnum was giving in Hartford. He continued his speech to the General Assembly without disclosing the devastating information.

P. T. BARNUM

What: An overlooked legacy of The Greatest Showman

Where: Barnum Museum, 820 Main St., Bridgeport

Cost: N/A

Noteworthy: Bridgeport's Barnum Museum is closed for renovations and object restoration following several natural disasters.

Photographic portrait of P. T. Barnum, likely taken in 1865 when he was first elected to the Connecticut General Assembly. Collection of the Barnum Museum, Bridgeport, Connecticut. Photo courtesy of The Barnum Museum, Bridgeport, Connecticut.

Barnum invented the attractions industry and lived up to his reputation as The Greatest Showman. But an important part of his legacy is his determination to use his platform "to do what is right."

Barnum was vocal not only about emancipation and suffrage, but also temperance and the eradication of the death penalty.

SLOW DOWN AND PAY ATTENTION

Why is the Merritt Parkway considered a national treasure?

It might seem odd to think of a road that gets you from Point A to Point B as a carefully planned work of art, but the Merritt Parkway is just that. Landscaped with nearly 200,000 shrubs and trees, the parkway had 46 wide curves with panoramic countryside views of ponds and meadows. Before black tar, the road originally was white concrete that blended with the original 72 individually designed Neoclassical, Art Deco, and Moderne concrete bridges. It was an aesthetically pleasing open road, perfect for a Sunday afternoon drive.

The "Queen of Parkways" relieved pressure on the colonial-era Boston Post Road from an ever-increasing motoring populace. Open to traffic in 1938, it was 37 ½ miles long and connected nine towns and cities full of civic-minded residents who cared about aesthetics. The sculptor of Mount Rushmore, Gutzon Borglum, insisted that Stamford's Rippowam River Bridge, which faced his yard, be stone-faced.

A father-and-son sculptor team, Febo and Edward Ferrari, carved Puritan and Native American scenes on the Comstock Hill Avenue Bridge in Norwalk; Yale-trained Edward also is responsible for the cobwebs and spiders and delicate concrete and iron butterflies on Fairfield's Merwins Lane Bridge. The Park Avenue Bridge in Trumbull was modeled after Venice's Rialto

If you get nostalgic about paying tolls, you can visit the road's former tollbooths in Stratford's Boothe Park and at the Henry Ford Museum in Dearborn, Michigan.

The Merritt Parkway was carefully planned with attention to aesthetic details like artistic bridges and lush landscaping. Photo courtesy of Library of Congress.

Bridge, and cast-iron grapevines spread across the Lake Avenue underpass in Greenwich.

Even the service stations were thoughtfully designed, with a bay window and exterior lanterns, and ladies' rooms featured bottle warmers and a weekend attendant specifically tasked to help mothers with young children.

So slow down and observe why the Merritt Parkway is a National Scenic Byway, a State Scenic Road, and on the National Register of Historic Places.

MERRITT PARKWAY

What: A model parkway

Where: Greenwich to Stratford

Cost: Free

Noteworthy: The surveying and construction of the bridges are remembered for eternity on Fairfield's Burr Street Bridge, which depicts men at work.

DON'T MESS WITH CONNECTICUT

What did Eli Whitney invent besides the cotton gin?

"We built the first American warship and the first ballistic-missile submarine, and we invented floating mines, underwater torpedoes, the repeating rifle, Gatling gun, automatic pistol, gun silencer, and bazooka rocket gun," Charles Monaghan wrote in *Connecticut Icons*, referencing *Connecticut Firsts* by Wilson Faude and Joan Friedland.

Connecticut got the nickname "Arsenal of the Nation" during the Revolutionary War for supplying the Continental Army, and it never looked back. At the Museum of Connecticut History, one room holds every gun made at Samuel Colt's Hartford factory, as well as firearms manufactured by 23 different Connecticut companies including Winchester, Sharps, and Marlin.

Schoolchildren learn that Eli Whitney invented the cotton gin, but another of his revolutionary inventions is not as well-known. When others made their own cotton-processing engines using his method, Whitney was almost financially ruined fighting legal battles. In manufacturing the cotton gin he found that if workers made the same parts over and over again instead of making entire machines, the process went faster.

He applied this idea of using standardized, interchangeable machine-made parts to making weapons, and the government gave him a contract for 10,000 firearms. "When he signed the

COLT'S NEW MODEL ARMY METALLIC CARTRIDGE REVOLVING PISTOL.

The Drawing is one-half the size of the Pistol.
cal. .45 inch.   Price $20.00.

COLT'S METALLIC CARTRIDGE ARMY PISTOL, W

Eli Whitney founded a weapons factory using machine-made interchangeable parts, a time-saving invention adopted by other gun manufacturers such as Colt, and other industries. Photos courtesy of Library of Congress.

WHITNEY'S IMPROVED FIRE-ARMS.

contract, Whitney had no factory, no workers and no experience in gun manufacturing," according to eliwhitney.org. He set up a factory in Hamden where "he developed a filing jig, a drilling machine, a milling machine, trip hammers, and other labor-saving devices, all power-driven," according to Nancy Finlay, writing for connecticuthistory.org.

Other companies making products like clocks adopted his system of mass production, and Whitney now is credited as constructing the first American factory.

Simeon North worked in Middletown at the same time as Whitney, making pistols for the government by using machines and a division of labor.

THE STATE'S STEPFORD LEGACY

Doesn't your home have a Moorish Room, 42-foot rotunda, and murals of frolicking Cupids?

Building flashy dream houses and satirizing the suburbs are nothing new. Le Grand Lockwood constructed his stunner in 1868, and more than a century later it was the setting for men who built not only houses but also wives to order.

Ira Levin spun a tale of husbands in the idyllic town of Stepford, Connecticut who killed their wives and replaced them with physically flawless and submissive robotic versions who never nagged, burned the roast, or raised their voices. The title of his 1972 best seller, *The Stepford Wives*, became a catchphrase for suburban housewives who strive for the ideal body and domestic life at the expense of independent thought and achievement. Fascination with the thriller led to two film adaptions (1975 and 2004), and the location scouts found no shortage of options in the state to play the parts of perfect home, perfect town green, and perfect Stepford Wife

LOCKWOOD-MATHEWS MANSION

What: *Stepford Wives* mansion

Where: 295 West Ave., Norwalk

Cost: Free–$10

Noteworthy: Lockwood died only four years after moving in; the Mathews family lived here from 1876 to 1938.

extra. Levin based Stepford on Wilton, where he once lived, and towns like New Canaan and Darien made celluloid appearances, but the location star of both films is a massive, turreted Victorian in Norwalk.

Noteworthy in scale and ambition, the 62-room Lockwood-Mathews Mansion is an imposing mix of Victorian, French

Norwalk's imposing Lockwood-Mathews Mansion is the cinematic location of the Stepford Men's Club in both the 1975 and 2004 Stepford Wives *films. Photo courtesy of Steve Turner, David Scott Parker Architects.*

Chateau, and Scottish Manor architecture with an interior richly decorated with frescoes, gilt, and marble. Such is the setting for the films' Stepford Men's Club, where the dastardly husbands transform their wives. The mansion has held many private events over the years, but the director guarantees that there is no robotic workshop in the basement.

The original estate was surrounded by 30 acres landscaped under the direction of William Trubee, the building supervisor of P. T. Barnum's house, Iranistan.

THE MYSTERIOUS CRITTER THAT STARTED A CRAZE

Why would you want to punch a nauga?

"Punch him in the nose the minute he comes through the door. Spill a Bloody Mary on him. Get him with a pie in the face. Smear chocolate on his chest. Kick him around," instructed a November 1967 ad. Why would you want to attack a cute little nauga? Because he doesn't mind the abuse; he's indestructible, according to the advertising firm that first introduced naugas to the American public in 1966, hoping they'd sell Naugahyde®. The warm and fuzzy campaign and nauga dolls were meant to make people less wary about an industrial fabric, and it worked. The ads started a cultural phenomenon. Johnny Carson interviewed a nauga on his late-night talk show, a reference showed up in the *Garfield* comic strip, and comedians crafted whole routines around the elusive beast. Americans got caught up in a cryptozoological craze on the same level as Sasquatch.

Naugahyde® first was produced in 1920 at the US Rubber plant in Naugatuck. One of the original 12 stocks in the Dow Jones Industrial Average, the company was founded in 1892, became Uniroyal Corp. in 1964, and now is located in Wisconsin.

PUTTING THE NAUGA IN NAUGAHYDE®

What: Elusive creatures that give their "hydes" for Naugahyde®

Where: Secret protected habitat on a Stoughton, WI ranch

Cost: $14.95–$39.95

Noteworthy: There's a nauga now that comes with a removable mask, because naugas are susceptible to COVID-19, too.

A 1960s advertising campaign successfully introduced the nauga to America to sell Naugahyde®, an artificial leather. Photo courtesy of x-ray delta one James Vaughan.

Naugas were rumored to be native to Sumatra and endangered, due to the popularity of their use in office furniture; their footstool-shaped children were studied and named uglettes.

The truth about these elusive creatures is made clear on the Uniroyal website, where you can "adopt" a nauga: "NAUGAs are bred in an incredibly wide variety of colors at our Stoughton, WI ranch, but they shed randomly for the creation of our NAUGA Dolls."

So there's no need to join the Save the Nauga! letter-writing campaign. No naugas are hurt in the production of Naugahyde®.

The world's first rubber-based artificial leather, Naugahyde® became widespread in the transportation industry and expanded to footwear, clothing, and luggage. When the company branched out to home furnishings, the nauga was born.

A WALK THROUGH THE STATE'S MILITARY HISTORY

Interested in some World War II SPAM® or the wing of a Japanese Zero?

In West Haven you can walk inside a bunker, sit in a Jeep with a 50-caliber mounted machine gun, and see a rare example of a Civil War Union frock coat. The under-the-radar West Haven Veterans Museum and Learning Center collects and interprets the state's military history through the lens of the 102nd Infantry Regiment. And it's a long history.

Benedict Arnold was a hero when he led a unit of militia and Governors Foot Guard volunteers, and his actions explain why Powder House Day is reenacted in New Haven every April. Unique and rare Civil War objects include unearthed battlefield artifacts and an autograph book with the signatures of William Tecumseh Sherman and President William McKinley. There are several World War I doughboy uniforms and the only known portrait of the canine Sergeant Stubby, who captured the hearts of the nation.

World War II stories are told through both Allied and Axis artifacts, including the wing of an infamous Japanese Zero plane shot down by the Branford 211th anti-aircraft artillery unit, a display of rations, and the wedding gown a bride made from the parachute that saved her groom.

The New Haven Grays fought in 19 Civil War battles, including the Battle of Bull Run and Gettysburg; see a replica of their elegant room.

At the West Haven Veterans Museum and Learning Center, you can sit in a Jeep, walk into a bunker, and see a replica of the New Haven Gray's elegant room. Photo courtesy of West Haven Veterans Museum and Learning Center.

Here, you can enter full-scale replicas of Officers' Quarters and a Korean War bunker, learn about a female Vietnamese spy, understand how communications equipment worked, and see weapons including a 1917 Browning .30-caliber, a water-cooled machine gun and a French 75-mm cannon.

So if you want to learn about two Chinese-Americans who fought in the Civil War, what a Gibson Girl transmitter did, and how uniforms changed through the centuries, head to this warehouse space by the train station and support the efforts of these keepers of Connecticut's proud military history.

WEST HAVEN VETERANS MUSEUM

What: Military museum

Where: 30 Hood Terr., West Haven

Cost: Free; donations accepted.

Noteworthy: The center has more than 1,000 military history books, including rare firsthand accounts by soldiers who served in the Revolutionary War through current conflicts.

WHAT IN THE WORLD IS A GUNGYWAMP?

What are those rock formations in the woods?

There are approximately 5,500 known archaeology sites in Connecticut, many relating to the state's early inhabitants, from before contact with Europeans. One that has drawn wide attention is Gungywamp, on state-owned and privately owned land in Groton, so it can only be accessed via official guided tours.

Often, wooded archaeological sites are unobtrusive to the untrained eye, and easy to walk past without realizing their history and significance. Many of Gungywamp's structures are more apparent; some date to the colonial era and others much earlier. Rock overhangs provided shelter to early people; shards of pottery and remnants of stone implements show evidence of use by paleo (ancient) and woodland Native Americans. There are vestiges of colonial homes and rock walls, and a row of standing stones is thought to have been an early American sheep pen. A sod-covered beehive arrangement of stones is called a Calendar Chamber, because an opening allows in daylight during the spring and fall equinoxes.

In Barkhamsted there's an Indian cave and soapstone quarry dating to 800 BCE. Here, under rock ledges, Native Americans excavated soapstone and carved bowls—there's even a discernible form of a bowl left under construction.

Washington's Templeton Site is a 10,000-year-old tool-making camp; Naugatuck's Binette Rock Shelter shows

In 1995, the state returned Fort Shantok State Park to the Mohegan Nation; it's now part of the Mohegan Reservation.

Archaeological sites like Groton's Gungywamp and Fort Shantok in Montville inform our understanding of how people before us lived. Photo courtesy of Bulletin of the Archaeological Society of Connecticut Digital Archive.

Photo Courtesy of Mills Photograph Collection of Connecticut, Connecticut Illustrated, Connecticut Digital Archive.

evidence of human use from paleo-Indians to 18th-century European American travelers. The Mohegan fort, village, and burial ground at Fort Shantok in Montville is the place Sachem Uncas first settled the tribe, and it's the site of a 1645 battle with the Narragansetts.

GOING WAY BACK

What: Archaeological sites

Where: Various

Cost: Free

Pro Tip: Follow the Office of State Archaeology on Facebook to keep informed about their projects and programming.

Especially when there are no primary sources—like eyewitness testimonies or written records—archaeological studies provide valuable information about the state's early residents.

NO BORING ARTIFACTS HERE

What do a two-headed calf and Steven Spielberg have in common?

"A Calf with two complete heads; also a Pig of the same description having two perfect heads to one body," read an advertisement the Reverend Joseph Steward placed in the *Hartford Courant*'s May 9, 1804, edition to entice readers to his museum.

Reverend Steward's poor health did not allow him to preach, so when the State House was opening in 1796 he petitioned for a space for a "painting room." He meant a studio for himself, but unfortunately his paintings were described as "wretched," so he switched gears and created a museum of "natural and artificial curiosities."

People came to see "the largest Bengal tiger ever seen," an English weather station, "a number of beautiful birds and other animals from the island of Japan," "a sword from a sword-fish four feet in length," "a large historic painting of Thomas Paine, and of Voltaire." The two-headed calf was big sensation, and a replacement can be seen today.

Steward's displays were popular, and in 1808 he moved his museum to an extension he built on his house nearby. When he died in 1822, the museum closed but was reopened from 1824 to 1840 under group ownership. Barnum's American Museum opened in 1841, and the Wadsworth Atheneum (Daniel

Steven Spielberg's 1997 movie *Amistad* recreated the actual courtroom in the Old State House where a trial took place.

A two-headed calf like the one that brought many visitors to Reverend Joseph Steward's original museum is among the oddities and curiosities on display at the recreated museum in the Old State House. Photo courtesy of Image Marketing Consultants.

Wadsworth was one of the men behind Steward's post-mortem museum) in 1844, so it seems as if Steward inspired these gentlemen.

The 1992 restoration of the Charles Bulfinch-designed Old State House included a recreation of Joseph Steward's Hartford Museum. Now on the second floor, its "oddities and curiosities" include a giant crocodile and Stewart's own portraits, so you can judge his talent for yourself.

JOSEPH STEWARD'S MUSEUM

What: One of America's earliest museums

Where: Connecticut's Old State House, 800 Main St., Hartford

Cost: Free–$8

Pro Tip: Don't miss the Gilbert Stuart portrait of George Washington that hangs in the location where it was originally intended.

NO THROWING STONES

Is there anything else to see besides a glass house at the Glass House?

Of course, visitors come to the Glass House to see the house. Not widely known: There are 14 structures on the property's 49 acres.

The glass walls and open floor plan of the stunning yet simple Glass House, a mere 55 feet long and 33 feet wide, were revolutionary when Philip Johnson moved in, in 1949. Known for numerous Manhattan skyscrapers, Johnson was architecture department director at the Museum of Modern Art and won the first Pritzker Architecture Prize in 1979.

Johnson referred to the sculpture gallery on the grounds, which features works by Robert Rauschenberg and Frank Stella, as "the best single room that I have ever designed." Carved into a hill, a bunker-like art gallery displays rotating exhibitions, and there's also a brick guest house, a mini-castle-like studio, and a tiny Ghost House, which the architect created because he was bored looking at just trees from his study. He added the red, non-linear Da Monsta in 1995.

GLASS HOUSE

What: The groundbreaking home of a noted architect

Where: The Glass House Visitor Center, 199 Elm St., New Canaan

Cost: Free–$250

Pro Tip: Tours start across the street from the Metro-North train station in downtown New Canaan, full of restaurants and stores.

How do you handle the design of a bathroom in a glass house? The small, circular bathroom—which includes a toilet, sink, and shower—is enclosed and obfuscated.

The glass walls and open floor plan of the Glass House were revolutionary when Philip Johnson moved in, in 1949. There are 14 structures on the artistically landscaped property, including a guest house and a sculpture gallery. Photo courtesy of Steve Healy.

The landscape also is a Johnson-designed work of art. He cut trees and built bridges, dug a pond and in it placed an island with a half-scale "pavilion" reminiscent of his design for Lincoln Center's New York State Theater. By the pond, he built a 30-foot sculptural tower that was meant to be climbed.

The Glass House is interesting for many reasons, not least of all the fact that it's more than a glass house.

AHOY, MATEY!

Did Captain Kidd bury treasure in Connecticut?

Naming a secret location of buried treasure Money Point or Money Island probably isn't too wise. Legends of the lost Connecticut treasure of Captain William Kidd have been passed down for hundreds of years, with secret booty rumored to be hidden on Charles Island, off Milford's Silver Sands Beach; in an underwater cave on Money Island, one of the Thimbles; and at Lion's Rock in Old Lyme, among others. Then, there are Money Points in Westbrook, Stonington, and Mystic.

Kidd walked the line between pirate and privateer, claiming booty for himself or for a country that engaged him. In 1698, Kidd seized a sizable vessel, *Quedagh Merchant*, that was laden with gold, silver, silk, and spices. The ruler of the Indian Mughal Empire didn't take kindly to the loss of these valuable goods and complained to the British East India Company, which marked Kidd as a pirate.

Kidd passed through the Caribbean and Gardiners Island on his way to Boston, where he was arrested and charged with piracy and murder. The Scotsman was repatriated to England and hanged in 1701.

The legend of his buried Connecticut treasure begins with actual treasure he left on Gardiners Island, which is close to the Connecticut coast. Kidd asked to keep treasure there in 1699 but it was needed as evidence in his trial. How much of it was returned? The Gardiners claim several family heirlooms and

BURIED TREASURE

What: Captain Kidd's treasure

Where: Wouldn't we all like to know?

Cost: Priceless

Noteworthy: England gave the Gardiners, original Connecticut settlers, their island in 1639. It's remained private property in the same family, and became part of New York in 1655.

Captain Kidd walked the line between state-sanctioned privateer and rogue pirate, paying the ultimate price for his plunders after seizing a ship that carried treasures the Indian government claimed. Photo courtesy of the Library of Congress.

even a sack of sugar as remnants of Kidd's booty. Evidence has not been found across the Sound, but that doesn't stop each generation from searching. Unfortunately, this is one secret of Connecticut that this author has not uncovered.

Milford hosts a pirate festival every year with residents of all ages dressing the part, cheering on "Captain Kidd" in Milford Harbor, and joining a treasure (scavenger) hunt.

LOOKS CAN BE DECEIVING

What's so special about this house?

At first glance, the Austin House looks like a stylized version of any number of mansions in the state, but a closer look reveals an intriguing architectural secret and two floors with wildly divergent design philosophies.

The house is only 18 feet deep. Long and narrow, the 86-foot Neoclassical Revival home was inspired by a 16th-century Italian villa the owners admired on their honeymoon. The lushly detailed Rococo first floor engulfs visitors in elegance, with gilded furniture and walls adorned with 18th-century Venetian silk. A sparse and radically modern International Style second floor includes a black linoleum floor, black bathtub, different colored walls, chrome Marcel Breuer furniture, chrome light fixtures, and chrome lever door handles.

The residents were Helen Goodwin Austin and A. Everett ("Chick") Austin, Jr., the pioneering director of the nearby Wadsworth Atheneum from 1927 to 1944, founder of Trinity College's fine arts department, and an all-around arts impresario. He was the first in America to produce a comprehensive Pablo Picasso exhibition and to present an opera with an all-Black cast. Thanks to Austin, another creative visionary, George Balanchine, left an incredible legacy in the United States. Austin sponsored Balanchine's relocation from Russia to found the School of American Ballet in Hartford, but

Helen Goodwin donated the house to the Wadsworth Atheneum in 1985. It's a National Historic Landmark and the largest object in the Wadsworth's collection.

The home built by the director of the Wadsworth Atheneum has two surprising secrets. Photo courtesy of Gene Gaddis, Wadsworth Atheneum.

AUSTIN HOUSE

What: An unusual home with an important arts legacy

Where: 130 Scarborough St., Hartford

Cost: Free–$15

Noteworthy: America's oldest art museum, the Wadsworth Atheneum, is well known for its Hudson River School collection and houses the Amistad Center for Art and Culture.

his residence was fleeting and the company evolved into the New York City Ballet.

To be a fly on the wall at the Austins' parties . . . they entertained Philip Johnson and Le Corbusier, Agnes de Mille and Martha Graham, George Gershwin and Aaron Copland, Salvador Dali and Alexander Calder.

In his museum and his home, Austin combined the classical with the avant garde. He left a creative legacy and a skinny home.

THERE'S NOTHING EVIL IN THE DARK FOREST

How did an internet legend begin?

A town that's not a town, a paranormal legend with no basis, a litigious homeowners' group out for blood. Put them all together and you get Dudleytown, the real name of a part of Cornwall that has a century of rumors to dispel.

It all started with two pages of sensationalist and invented portrayals of residents in the 1926 *A History of Cornwall, Connecticut: A Typical New England Town* by Edward C. Starr. He described townspeople afflicted by insanity and unnatural death, but neither the Cornwall Historical Society nor Dudleytown residents—some who have lived there for generations—have identified any basis for supernatural activity, either then or since.

In the 18th century, residents with the last name Dudley lent their name to a southwestern area of Cornwall on a hill. They felled trees to farm, but by 1920 more than half of the population left to follow other fortunes and homestead in the West.

The land then became a private forest. Wanting to escape city life and promote conservation, in 1924, 41 New Yorkers bought 800 acres and planted 4,000 trees. The Dark Entry Forest Association kept planting trees on Bald Mountain, snubbing the mountain's name with 10,000 trees by 1927. The newly forested

---

DUDLEYTOWN

What: A legend debunked

Where: Cornwall Historical Society, 7 Pine St., Cornwall

Cost: Free

Pro Tip: Residents' fingers are poised to dial the police, so don't even think of heading to these quiet woods in search of Starr's legend.

Cornwall's covered lattice truss bridge over the Housatonic River, built circa 1864, is one of many appealing area attractions. Photo courtesy of Anastasia Mills Healy.

residential community hosted summer camps for children and in the winter attracted skiers.

When supernatural stories spread on the internet, Dudleytown residents buckled down to protect their property from ghost hunters who trespassed, vandalized, and further spread rumors.

Move on . . . nothing to see here. Check out the beautiful covered bridge, take a walk in the public Mohawk State Forest, or visit the Cornwall Historical Society to learn the truth about the area.

Starr was a Yale-trained minister whose town research formed the basis of the collections of the Cornwall Historical Society. His motivation to include false information about residents is lost to history.

THE MYSTERY OF THE LEATHERMAN

Who was he, and why did he walk a constant 365-mile loop?

Beginning in 1883, people in towns as distant as Woodbury and Mount Kisco, New York, realized that they were getting a regular visitor. A man dressed head to toe in roughly stitched leather clothing appeared predictably every 34 days.

People asked questions, but he did not speak. No one ever learned who he was, where he was from, or why he constantly was walking a 365-mile, clockwise route through Connecticut and New York.

He never asked for food or lodging and was not a nuisance. In fact, people anticipated his appearance, greeted him, and gave him food, which he accepted.

In the heat of summer and through winter snowdrifts, he continued this route, wearing an estimated 60 pounds of leather and sleeping in caves and rock shelters.

To feed curiosity and sell papers, a newspaper published a story about him that stated he was a Frenchman named Jules Bourglay who failed miserably working at a tannery to impress a woman, and now, as penance, wandered in a foreign land wearing leather. The paper later admitted to fabricating the story, but other papers had picked it up and the false

New Haven's East Rock Brewing Co. produces Leatherman Beer; Pearl Jam wrote a song about him; and there's an annual 10k Leatherman's Loop race in Cross River, New York.

Wearing and carrying an estimated 60 pounds of leather, the mysterious man known as The Leatherman walked a constant 365-mile route, appearing in a set number of towns every 34 days (all without an Apple Watch). Photo courtesy of the Connecticut Historical Society.

story spread. The Leatherman died from cancer at age 50 and is buried at Sparta Cemetery in Ossining, New York. More recently, after years of research, Dan DeLuca postulated in *The Old Leather Man* that this itinerant was a French Canadian who knew Native American culture.

THE LEATHERMAN

What: Mysterious traveling vagabond

Where: Various

Cost: Free

Pro Tip: Check out Lee-Stuart Evans's *Air Land and Sea* blog for how to find the Leatherman's caves.

A British athlete, Lee-Stuart Evans, traced Leatherman's route in 2019, walking 343 miles in nine days. He remarked: "This wasn't a mad man in the woods, this was a master woodsman living in perfectly selected caves, with nearby water, cultivated herb gardens and stacked fire wood."

BEFORE THERE WAS BERNIE

Why was America's most beloved pediatrician also the most despised?

We all have Dr. Spock (the pediatrician, not the Vulcan) to thank for being cuddled as babies. Before Dr. Benjamin Spock's 1946 *The Common Sense Book of Baby and Child Care*, parents were instructed not to show too much affection, for fear of spoiling their children. Spock told parents to trust their instincts, let kids be kids, and to ease up on strict schedules.

These parents of Baby Boomers had a lot of children on their hands, and his book sold like wildfire.

It's remained in print, selling 50 million copies in 40 languages.

What is surprising about this New Haven native and globally beloved pediatrician is that he was a vocal socialist who, in 1972, ran for president on a platform of free college education and health care, legalizing abortion and marijuana, and the issue he cared about most: nuclear disarmament.

Spock was active in the National Committee for a Sane Nuclear Policy (now Peace Action), which worked to quash nuclear weapons. He supported civil rights and marched with Dr. Martin Luther King Jr., who also was anti-nuke. National sentiment rose against Spock, who was accused of corrupting the youth of America and was arrested dozens of times. In 1968, he was charged with encouraging draft resistance, but his sentence was dropped.

THE NON-VULCAN DR. SPOCK

What: A trusted pediatrician who became a reviled socialist

Where: Worldwide

Cost: N/A

Noteworthy: Spock won a gold medal in rowing at the 1924 Olympic Games.

The pediatrician and bestselling author, Dr. Benjamin Spock, ran for president as a socialist on a platform that included free education and free healthcare like his doppleganger Bernie Sanders. Photo courtesy of Warren K. Leffler, Library of Congress.

Dr. Spock continued to campaign for peace and disarmament until his death at 94, saying "There's no point in raising children if they're going to be burned alive."

As director of the Boston's Children's Museum for 23 years, Dr. Spock's son, Michael, popularized the concept of hands-on, experiential exhibits.

LOOK OUT BEHIND YOU!

Why are there Dilophosauruses in the dome and Brachiosaurs in the bushes?

Don't be alarmed, but herds of carnivorous Jurassic Dilophosauruses have been spotted in Rocky Hill, and 50 building-size dinosaurs are occupying Montville.

About 200 million years ago, Rocky Hill ostensibly was teeming with dinosaurs, based on the 2,600 footprints uncovered by a construction crew in 1966. Built around this discovery of one of the world's largest dinosaur trackways, Dinosaur State Park enables viewing of 750 of these prints in an interpretive center under a geodesic dome; the rest are buried for preservation.

In the domed realm of the dinosaurs, the 20-foot Dilophosaurus stalks its prey in the mudflats, while the smaller Anchisaurus feeds on ferns. Dimorphodon, a carnivorous flying reptile with a four-foot wingspan, hovers overhead.

There are hands-on activities at the Dig Pit and Discovery Room, plus geocaching, track casting, gem and fossil mining, and an arboretum with cedar of Lebanon and giant sequoia.

Meanwhile, in Montville, come face to foot with 50 life-sized dinosaurs that tower over the tree-lined trails at Dinosaur Place. Flat, wide, and good for strollers, the 1 ½ miles of trails circle a lake and wind past an erupting volcano and two caves, where animatronic dinosaurs (including a Dilophosaurus) growl at the curious.

A dinosaur and its footprints are named independently: the Dilophosaurus is thought to have left Eubrontes tracks.

There are thousands of real dinosaur footprints in Rocky Hill and 50 life-sized dinosaur models in Montville. Photo courtesy Dinosaur State Park.

Photo by Dinosaur Place at Nature's Art Village.

Ever wanted to take a selfie with a 40-foot tall Brachiosaurus or hug an armored Euoplocephalus? Here's your chance.

At the 60-acre complex, kids also can climb the T-Rex Tower at the playground, work on their putting at mini-golf, navigate a maze, dig for gems, pan for gold, unearth fossils, and cool off in summer at a splash pad—all dinosaur-themed.

So whether you enter the real Land of the Lost or the Hollywood version, you'll see that there's not only colonial history in Connecticut—the time machine goes back way farther.

ROAR!

What: Dinosaurs!

Where: Dinosaur State Park, 400 West St., Rocky Hill

Dinosaur Place at Nature's Art Village, 1650 Hartford New London Tpke., Montville

Cost: Nature's Art Village: Free–$23.99; Dinosaur State Park: Free–$6

Pro Tip: To take home one of the coolest souvenirs ever, come prepared with the items listed on Dinosaur State Park's website to make a track cast.

ELEMENTARY, MY DEAR . . .

What castle-dwelling actor is responsible for Sherlock Holmes's most famous phrase?

You know an actor with 17 cats who conducts his own private railroad is going to build a unique house. His will instructed that it "not be sold to some blithering saphead."

An itinerant stage actor for much of his career, William Gillette would share a sandwich with each resident theater feline and scrapbook their photos. He threw birthday parties for his own cats and collected cat figurines.

Guests, including Albert Einstein, President Calvin Coolidge, and Charlie Chaplin, joined Gillette for a spin on the narrow-gauge railroad he built on his 122-acre property, complete with bridges, turnarounds, and a tunnel; Lake Compounce visitors rode it around the lake from 1943 to 1991.

Gillette was a practical joker. He used a hidden stairwell door for surprise entrances and exits and designed his 14,000-square-foot home with strategically placed mirrors to spy on guests. He tucked a well-concealed second tower room in the servants' stairwell, accessed via vertical stairs with a locking mechanism, and purposefully designed the stone roof to look like a ruin. Another fun fact: His friend and head of staff, Yukitaka Osaki, was the brother of the mayor of Tokyo who gifted Washington, DC, its cherry trees.

WILLIAM GILLETTE

What: Unique home with a Sherlock Holmes connection

Where: Gillette Castle State Park, 67 River Rd., East Haddam

Cost: Park free; castle free–$6

Pro Tip: Pay attention to the handcrafted doors: Gillette designed all 47 to be different, each with unique external latches.

William Gillette's castle-like home is open to the public for tours and is part of a state park. Photo courtesy of Kelly Hunt Cherish the Moment Photography.

However, what will be most surprising and compelling to many is that it was Gillette who wrote the first authorized Sherlock Holmes adaptation for the stage, who came up with Holmes's catchphrase "Elementary, my dear fellow" (which evolved into ". . . my dear Watson"), and who originated the character's deerstalker cap, curved pipe, and magnifying glass.

What actor played Holmes more than 1,300 times over the course of 33 years? Elementary, my dear reader.

Mark Twain bought land from Gillette's father to build his Hartford home. The families were friends, and Twain helped Gillette early in his career.

PUTTING THE "WOODS" IN FOXWOODS

Did you know that the casino is surrounded by 2,000 acres of forest?

The "woods" part of Foxwoods is surprising to many, as is its zipline and an observation tower many people miss at its extraordinary museum.

Follow the fox paw prints in the Great Cedar Casino Lobby and take a trail to the Mashantucket Pequot Museum, a scenic loop behind the Two Trees Inn, or the more challenging Lantern Hill Trail, where, from its 500-foot peak, Block Island Sound can be discerned on a clear day.

There are three options to see the woods from above. Adrenaline junkies won't hesitate to jump off the rooftop of Fox Tower and zoom up to 60 miles per hour on the HighFlyer Zipline. At 350 feet, the travel is high above the treeline, and with a distance of 3,750 feet, it's the longest zipline in Connecticut. The higher floors of the casino buildings offer great views; if staying overnight, ask for a room in the Grand Pequot Tower with floor-to-ceiling windows overlooking 2,000 acres of forest, as far as the eye can see.

Then, there's the 185-foot observation tower at the Mashantucket Pequot Museum. Hawks circle past the small, glassed-in tower; taken from this height, photos of the Foxwoods complex in the distance, past the forest, look like

---

FOXWOODS

What: Casino in a forest

Where: Foxwoods, 350 Trolley Line Blvd., Mashantucket

Cost: Various

Pro Tip: At the museum, opt for the escalator for a descent into the Ice Age, complete with faux glaciers overhead and running water, setting the scene for the story of the Mashantucket Pequots.

From the observation tower at the Mashantucket Pequot Museum, it's apparent that Foxwoods is surrounded by 2,000 acres of forest. Photo courtesy of Anastasia Mills Healy.

postcards. When visitors arrive at the main museum entrance, the ticket booth is straight ahead and the entrance to the tower is behind, so many people overlook it. A highlight of the massive museum itself is a realistically recreated village from thousands of years ago.

So, just like Las Vegas casinos have circuses, canals, and beaches, Foxwoods actually has woods—connected via zipline to a noteworthy museum with a spectacular view.

Spanning nine million square feet, Foxwoods has five casinos, four hotels, 3,400 slots, 249 table games, two spas, two theaters, two golf courses, and six nightclubs.

CONNECTICUT'S SWEET TOOTH

What well-known candy is produced in Connecticut?

You wouldn't necessarily think of chocolate as being patriotic, but now imagine that you're a colonist who's boycotting tea. Christopher Leffingwell opened Connecticut's first chocolate mill in 1770 on the Yantic River in Norwich; cacao beans were sourced from the Caribbean, not through England.

Nobody eats Leffingwell chocolate today, but a later Connecticut chocolatier still is popular worldwide. Peter Halajian started selling the Mounds Bar in 1921 and Almond Joy in 1948, in addition to other confections manufactured at the Peter Paul plant in Naugatuck. Cadbury Schweppes bought Peter Paul in 1978, and Hershey's bought Cadbury Schweppes ten years later—for $300 million! The Naugatuck plant closed in 2007, when operations moved to Virginia.

Now to semantics: The "Lolly Pop" was invented in Connecticut (not the "lollipop"). George Smith of New Haven's Bradley Smith Company started making hard candy on a stick in 1908, but didn't get a patent to call it a Lolly Pop until 1931. The delay was that "lollipop" was an English invention; Smith said he named his candy after a racehorse. Now, "lollipop" is generic.

Another candy didn't originate here but is produced in Orange: Pez. Ever wonder why they come in a dispenser that looks like a lighter? Pez (short for *pfefferminz*) was introduced in Vienna in 1927 to pop in your mouth, instead of a cigarette.

"Christopher Leffingwell Makes and sells Chocolate by the Quantity at his Shop in Norwich," read a 1771 newspaper ad. The Boston Tea Party happened two years later.

The world's largest PEZ dispenser, in the PEZ Visitor Center in Orange, stands just over 14 feet tall. The Orange factory produces an average of 12 million candy tablets every day. Photo courtesy of PEZ Candy, Inc.

The dispensers' heads and the collectible craze followed, beginning in 1955. The company started selling candy in the US in 1952, began manufacturing it in Connecticut in 1973, and opened the 4,000-square-foot visitor center in 2011. Between its locations in Orange and Traun, Austria, Pez produces 5 billion candies and 70 million dispensers per year. Brush your teeth, Connecticut!

HAVE IT MY WAY

What did New Haven men do that created a gastronomical phenomenon?

"This is not Burger King. You don't get it your way. You take it my way or you don't get the darned thing." That sign, plus the one with a ketchup bottle in a circle with a slash, are clues that Louis' Lunch stands on tradition, and that tradition does not include condiments.

From 1895 to 1907, Louis Lassen had a lunch wagon on Meadow Street in New Haven (then it moved to a permanent building). In 1889, William Perkins, who worked around the corner on Water Street for the New Haven Wire Goods Co. factory, received a patent for a gridiron to broil meat. Luigi Pieragostini, who worked at the company, had the idea to attach two gridirons, and invented a hinged broiler designed specifically for vertical stoves. Louis' Lunch still uses these same gas-powered, cast-iron, Bridge, Beach & Co. stoves, manufactured in 1898. Talk about seasoned cast iron!

In 1900, when a customer of Lassen's was in a rush and (according to legend) demanded, "Slap a meatpuck between two planks and step on it!" the hamburger sandwich was born. Note that a hamburger is served on a bun, whereas a hamburger sandwich is meat between two slices of bread. Louis' Lunch uses Pepperidge Farm (founded by a Fairfield

---

LOUIS' LUNCH

What: The first hamburger sandwich

Where: 261 Crown St., New Haven

Cost: $2–$7

Noteworthy: Louis' Lunch wagon served factory workers on Meadow Street, moved first to George Street and then to a purchased building, which the Lassens relocated to its present location in 1975 with the help of donations from loyal customers.

This famed burger spot started as a lunch wagon in 1895, and the cast-iron, vertical broilers that date to 1898 still are operated by the same family. Photo courtesy of Steve Healy.

woman) toasted white bread and offers only cheese, tomato, and onion as accompaniments. A secret mix of five meats is hand-rolled and cooked to order, and the patties are broiled the same way as they have been for generations. The chef's last name still is Lassen. I wonder if any Perkinses or Pieragostinis ever come by for a burger.

Vertical broilers cook meat evenly, simultaneously on both sides and use little counter space; rendered fat drips to the patties below, creating juicy burgers.

A TALE OF QUARANTINE AND STAR-CROSSED LOVERS

What is the tragic Revolutionary War love story of Elisha Benton and Jemima Barrows?

Elisha Benton and Jemima Barrows found themselves in quarantine in 1777. They wanted to start a life together, but his family, the Revolutionary War, and smallpox got in the way.

From one of Tolland's founding families, Daniel Benton built his red, Cape Cod, colonial, on 40 acres in 1720. His sons served in the French and Indian War; his grandsons, including the eldest, Elisha, fought in the American Revolution. Only Elisha returned, but his homecoming was bittersweet: he had contracted smallpox while being held on a British prison ship. At first there was good news—he was exchanged for a British prisoner and started the journey home from New York, where he had been captured in the Battle of Long Island. By the time he returned to Tolland, his fate was known, and he by law had to be kept from his loved ones, as there was no cure for smallpox.

At age 17, Barrows defied the order of quarantine and cared for Elisha until his death a few weeks after his return. She died five weeks later. Benton's father had disapproved of their union

> ## QUARANTINE LOVE STORY
>
> **What:** A Revolutionary War tale of love and death
>
> **Where:** Daniel Benton Homestead, 154 Metcalf Rd., Tolland
>
> **Cost:** Free
>
> **Noteworthy:** US Senator William Benton, who helped found the United Nations and published the *Encyclopedia Britannica*, is a descendant.

Elisha Benton, grandson of the home's builder, died from smallpox after returning from fighting the Revolutionary War. He was nursed by his formerly healthy young love, Jemima Barrows, who succumbed to smallpox soon after and is buried near him on the property. Photo courtesy of Tolland Historical Society.

due to her more modest circumstances, but agreed to unite them in death. However, unmarried couples could not be interred side by side. Today, visitors to the Daniel Benton Homestead can see Barrows' grave a few paces from Benton's.

Home to six generations of Bentons and countless triumphs and tragedies in its 300 years, the Daniel Benton Homestead is a reported site of paranormal activity. It might be the young lovers yearning for a reunion, or it could just be the creaks and rattles of an old home.

The Bentons imprisoned 20 Hessian soldiers in their cellar during the Revolutionary War; several settled in Tolland after the war ended.

SOURCES

20,000 Leagues Under the Connecticut River
https://connecticuthistory.org/david-bushnell-and-his-revolutionary-submarine/; https://www.
ussnautilus.org; https://lymeline.com/2020/01/a-view-from-my-porch-lyme-native-ezra-lee-
was-worlds-first-commander-of-an-attack-submarine-in-battle/

A Few Good Men
https://www.nlmaritimesociety.org/; https://www.nps.gov/subjects/travelamistad/stories.htm

A Camp for Adults
Clubgetaway.com

A Refuge in an Archipelago
http://outerisland.org/index.php?id=visit; https://www.friendsofouterisland.org/; https://www.
nytimes.com/2007/06/24/travel/24explorer.html

Adriaen Who?
https://www.courant.com/news/connecticut/hc-xpm-1998-05-24-9805240327-story.html;
https://www.newenglandhistoricalsociety.com/the-dutch-in-new-england-more-than-
sinterklaas-and-koekjes/

Ahoy, Matey!
Connecticut Pirates & Privateers Wick Griswold History Press 2015; https://www.
connecticutmag.com/history/the-pirates-of-long-island-sound/article_6d7860cb-4c0b-51b1-
9293-ba83fcbfefae.html; https://www.biography.com/explorer/william-kidd; https://www.
dailymail.co.uk/news/article-6878015/Gardiners-Island-mysterious-private-island-owned-
family-380-years-Hamptons-Captain-Kidd.html; https://www.newenglandhistoricalsociety.com/
william-kidd-vicious-pirate-enterprising-privateer/

America's First Spa Resort
https://www.newenglandhistoricalsociety.com/john-adams-has-a-spa-day-in-1771-at-
connecticuts-fashionable-stafford-springs/; https://www.courant.com/news/connecticut/hc-
xpm-1999-07-30-9907300381-story.html; https://www.history.com/news/10-things-you-should-
know-about-joseph-warren

A Mikvah in Montville
https://thebaronhirschcommunity.org/jewish-farmers-in-connecticut/; https://www.ctexplored.
org/hebrew-tillers-of-the-soil/; https://www.nps.gov/nr/feature/jewishheritage/2013/
Emanuel_Society_Synagogue_and_Creamery_Site.htm

A Quarter Acre of Heartache
https://bportlibrary.org/hc/south-end/the-golden-hill-paugussett-tribe/

An Island Retreat
https://www.endersisland.org/about

Back to the Future
https://www.phys.uconn.edu/~mallett/main/book.htm; https://en.wikipedia.org/wiki/Spike_
Lee%27s_unrealized_projects#Time_Traveler

Before Her Time
https://www.youtube.com/watch?v=x2GNvBsatTs&t=3s; https://portal.ct.gov/DECD/Content/
Historic-Preservation/04_State_Museums/Prudence-Crandall-Museum

Before There was Bernie
https://www.ncbi.nlm.nih.gov/pmc/articles/PMC3076385/

Berlin Graffiti
https://www.newenglandhistoricalsociety.com/glory-days-berlin-turnpike/; https://connecticuthistory.org/a-hip-road-trip/; https://www.nytimes.com/2001/02/18/nyregion/in-berlin-a-road-with-an-identity-crisis.html; https://en.wikipedia.org/wiki/American_Graffiti; Connecticut 169 Club, Martin Podskoch, Podskoch Press LLC, 2018.

Beyond the Hand Sock
https://drama.uconn.edu/programs/puppet-arts/facts/; www.bimp.uconn.edu

Boys Will Be Boys
https://www.greenwichtime.com/news/article/Boy-Scout-trail-Organization-can-trace-its-roots-3667758.php; https://oa-bsa.org/history/woodcraft-indians; https://americacomesalive.com/the-woodcraft-indians-ernest-thompson-seton-founder/; http://etsetoninstitute.org/influence-felt-around-the-world/seton-and-the-boy-scouts/

Brush Your Teeth
https://connecticuthistory.org/new-haven-gives-the-lollipop-its-name-today-in-history/; https://www.theday.com/article/20190203/ENT07/190209961; https://en.wikipedia.org/wiki/Peter_Paul_Candy_Manufacturing_Company

Calling All Scholars and Space Nuts
http://www.walkerdigital.com/the-walker-library_welcome.html; https://www.wired.com/2008/09/ff-walker/?currentPage=all; http://www.heritagecs.com/declaration.php

Connecticut's Stonehenge
https://www.edwardtufte.com/tufte/hogpen-hill-farms; https://www.ctexplored.org/hogpen-hill-farms-a-place-to-see/

Don't Mess With Connecticut
Connecticut Icons: Classic Symbols of the Nutmeg State By Charles Monagan; https://museumofcthistory.org/research-guide-colt-manufacturing-co/; https://www.eliwhitney.org/; https://connecticuthistory.org/north-and-south-the-legacy-of-eli-whitney/

Dreaming in Simsbury
https://www.mlkinct.com/documentary.html

Education Pioneers
https://www.asd-1817.org/about/history--cogswell-heritage-house; https://asd-1817.myschoolapp.com/ftpimages/1189/download/download_3129867.pdf; https://connecticuthistory.org/an-overview-of-connecticuts-outdoor-sculpture/

Elementary, My Dear . . .
https://www.gillettecastlefriends.org/; https://portal.ct.gov/DEEP/State-Parks/Parks/Gillette-Castle-State-Park; https://www.youtube.com/channel/UCrnlVQJXo8_6j7CFpyMJLmQ

First in Flight
http://www.gustave-whitehead.com/; https://airforces.fr/2016/08/14/gustave-whitehead-flew-on-august-14-1901/; http://ctmonuments.net/2012/11/gustave-whitehead-fountain-bridgeport/; https://www.nytimes.com/2015/04/18/nyregion/where-was-modern-flight-invented-connecticut-believes-it-holds-the-answer.html

The First US President was a Nutmegger
http://huntingtonhomestead.org/; https://www.newenglandhistoricalsociety.com/samuel-huntington-elected-presidentof-united-states/; https://guides.loc.gov/articles-of-confederation; https://history.house.gov/People/Continental-Congress/Presidents/

Firsts and Lasts in Bridgewater
https://www.bridgewatervillagestoreandbistro.com/story; https://www.nytimes.com/2018/09/19/realestate/bridgewater-conn-no-supermarkets-but-natural-beauty-to-spare.html; "Bridgewater Dry Town," Bridgewater Historical Society; https://npgallery.nps.gov/GetAsset/c7bd81af-bbcf-435e-98bd-3236bf41c237

The Freeman Sisters and Little Liberia
https://www.freemancenterbpt.org/houses.html; https://bportlibrary.org/hc/african-american-heritage/mary-and-eliza-freeman-houses/

Friends, Romans, Connecticans
https://ctstatelatinday.wordpress.com/; https://www.courant.com/hc-connecticut-state-latin-day-2015-20150501-photogallery.html

Frisbie!
https://www.frisbiepie.com/; https://www.toyhalloffame.org/toys/frisbee; https://www.atlasobscura.com/articles/frisbee-history; https://www.wfdf.org/history-stats/history-of-flying-disc/4-history-of-the-frisbee

Gatsby in Westport
"Boats Against the Current: The Honeymoon Summer of Scott and Zelda," Richard Webb, Jr. Prospecta Press, 2018; "Gatsby in Connecticut: The Untold Story" (2020)

The Golden Age of Comics on the Gold Coast
https://www.vanityfair.com/style/2017/08/when-fairfield-county-was-the-comic-strip-capital-of-the-world

Green Acres
https://www.ctexplored.org/frederick-law-olmsted-in-connecticut/

Have It My Way
https://louislunch.com/; http://www.americaslibrary.gov/es/ct/es_ct_burger_1.html; https://www.gearpatrol.com/food/a136913/louis-lunch-profile/; https://weirdeats.typepad.com/weirdeats/2007/01/burger_wars.html; https://connecticuthistory.org/louis-lunch-and-the-birth-of-the-hamburger/

Hidden Commentary
https://connecticuthistory.org/an-overview-of-connecticuts-outdoor-sculpture/; http://www.ct.gov/kids/lib/kids/pdf/connecticut_project_helper.pdf; https://commons.trincoll.edu/commons-2/artwork/paul-wayland-bartlett-equestrian-monument-to-the-marquis-de-lafayette/; http://ctmonuments.net/2013/10/lafayette-statue-hartford/; https://www.waymarking.com/waymarks/WMD540_The_Marquis_de_LaFayette_Hartford_CT; https://americanart.si.edu/artist/paul-wayland-bartlett-266; https://en.wikipedia.org/wiki/Apotheosis_of_Democracy; https://www.unjourdeplusaparis.com/en/paris-insolite/detail-insolite-statue-la-fayette; https://www.eutouring.com/images_paris_statues_533.html; https://equestrianstatue.org/lafayette-2/

Holy Mackerel
https://www.nps.gov/subjects/nationalhistoriclandmarks/upload/2020_fall_First-Presbyterian-Church.pdf

How to Make $4 Billion from Teapot Lids and Spare Bolts
https://archivessearch.lib.uconn.edu/repositories/2/resources/207; https://en.wikipedia.org/wiki/Frontier_Communications_of_Connecticut; https://about.att.com/innovation/ip/brands/history; https://en.wikipedia.org/wiki/AT%26T; https://connecticuthistory.org/the-first-commercial-telephone-exchange-today-in-history/; https://www.nps.gov/subjects/nationalhistoriclandmarks/site-of-the-first-telephone-exchange.htm

"I am no politician"
https://lostmuseum.cuny.edu/archive/p-t-barnums-speech-on-negro-suffrage-may-26-1; https://www.history.com/news/10-things-you-may-not-know-about-p-t-barnum

If It Flies, It Dies
https://www.fosa-ct.org/Reprints/Spring2016_NikeBase.htm; https://fas.org/nuke/guide/usa/airdef/nike-ajax.htm; http://coldwar-ct.com/Home_Page.php

I Have a Bridge to Sell You

Roebling Museum, Roebling, New Jersey; https://harpers.org/archive/2013/10/first-family-second-life/; "Rock Came From Here," *Greenwich Graphic*, June 25, 1926

Iranistan: Not a Former Soviet State
https://collections.ctdigitalarchive.org/islandora/object/60002%3A4013?search=iranistan; https://brightonmuseums.org.uk/royalpavilion/; https://www.ctpost.com/news/article/The-lost-palace-of-Iranistan-was-once-the-pride-11182198.php

The Ladies of Litchfield
arethusafarm.com; https://www.bostonglobe.com/lifestyle/travel/2016/09/01/choice-cream-from-coddled-cows/0MR19Oi7dct2y5s08YPYHI/story.html

Let Them Eat Grey Poupon
https://fairfieldcountylook.com/greenwich-landmarks-northway-1911/; https://halfpuddinghalfsauce.blogspot.com/2013/10/northway-residence-of-mr-and-mrs.html; http://en.chateauversailles.fr/sites/default/files/trianon_brochure_en_jan-2020-planche_bd.pdf

The Light on Ragged Mountain
conidubois.com; https://www.courant.com/news/connecticut/hc-xpm-1994-08-01-9408010020-story.html; https://www.connecticutmag.com/history/the-ct-files-the-barkhamsted-lighthouse/article_a874e24d-42bf-59f1-8c91-8bbded06bab6.html; https://todayincthistory.com/2018/12/03/december-3-the-barkhamsted-lighthouse/; http://www.ctmq.org/30-everybody-must-get-stoned/; https://www.iaismuseum.org/wp-content/uploads/2017/02/preserve-booklet-barkhamsted-lighthouse.pdf

Lone Eagle in Connecticut
United News Journal Vol. 5, No. 1, Jan-Feb 1991; https://www.darientimes.com/realestate2/article/On-the-Market-Charles-Lindbergh-s-onetime-12773321.php; http://www.ctmq.org/414-pratt-whitney-hangar-museum/

Look Out Behind You!
https://naturesartvillage.com/; https://portal.ct.gov/DEEP/State-Parks/Parks/Dinosaur-State-Park/; https://www.dinosaurstatepark.org/

Looks Can be Deceiving
https://www.thewadsworth.org/collection/austinhouse/; https://connecticuthistory.org/hartfords-facade-house-the-unique-home-of-chick-austin/; https://npgallery.nps.gov/GetAsset/ae9d37b1-f370-4525-a301-6ba9ab9fc377

Madame Butterfly on the Mianus
https://greenwichhistory.org/

Monets on the Mountain
https://www.hillstead.org/

Moving Mountains
https://www.holylandwaterbury.org/; http://www.waterburyobserver.org/wod7/node/3764; https://connecticuthistory.org/waterburys-holy-land/

The Mysterious Critter that Started a Craze
https://www.naugahyde.com/; https://www.smithsonianmag.com/smart-news/nauga-belgian-velcro-and-other-synthetic-creatures-180964811/; http://www.voicesofeastanglia.com/2012/08/nauga-the-vinyl-monster.html; https://www.snopes.com/fact-check/naugahyde-and-seek/

The Mystery of the Leatherman
https://connecticuthistory.org/the-old-leatherman-alive-in-our-memories/; https://hvmag.com/life-style/history/legend-in-leather/; https://theairlandandsea.com/2019/04/the-old-leatherman-caves-guide.html

Nazis Get NIMBYed

https://archives.rep-am.com/2012/11/11/elderly-woman-helped-rid-southbury-of-nazis-in-1937/; https://archives.rep-am.com/2018/04/29/southburys-defiance-of-nazis-in-holocaust-museum/; https://www.theatlantic.com/photo/2017/06/american-nazis-in-the-1930sthe-german-american-bund/529185/; http://www.americainwwii.com/articles/americans-for-hitler/

No Boring Artifacts Here

www.ctoldstatehouse.cga.ct.gov; "The Restoration of Joseph Steward's Hartford Museum" By Wilson H. Faude. *Antiques Magazine* October 2001; https://todayincthistory.com/2019/05/11/may-11-old-state-house-opens

No Lute Required

https://portal.ct.gov/About/State-Symbols/Connecticut-State-Troubadour; https://www.nekitawaller.com/; http://www.trob-eu.net/en

No Throwing Stones

https://theglasshouse.org/

O Little Town

https://christmastownfestival.com/around-town.html; https://abbeyofreginalaudis.org/ Connecticut Off the Beaten Path; https://www.courant.com/ctnow/hc-vann-shopping-around-1123-20141117-column.html; www.ci.bethlehem.ct.us/BPO.htm; https://www.smithsonianmag.com/arts-culture/a-creche-reborn-98867525/?no-ist

Our Own Indiana Jones

https://www.newenglandhistoricalsociety.com/hiram-bingham-connecticut-indiana-jones-stumbles-onto-machu-picchu/; https://todayincthistory.com/2018/07/24/july-24-hiram-bingham-iii-finds-machu-picchu/; https://www.ctexplored.org/discovering-the-explorer-hiram-bingham/; https://medium.com/@elanhead/an-explorer-in-the-air-service-b29b2364a4af; https://en.wikipedia.org/wiki/Hiram_Bingham_III

Putting the "woods" in Foxwoods

Foxwoods.com, www.pequotmuseum.org

Radiance Captured

www.marktwainhouse.org; http://www.tfaoi.com/aa/6aa/6aa425.htm; http://www.acswebnetworks.com/stjames-new/whoweare/article438038.htm; https://www.pequotchapel.org/history; https://www.lymanallyn.org/exhibitions/louis-comfort-tiffany-in-new-london/; https://www.courant.com/news/connecticut/hc-xpm-2003-12-14-0312140076-story.html

A Radiant Glow

http://www.waterburyobserver.org/wod7/node/2723; https://www.waterburyct.org/content/9586/9599/9604.aspx

Reuniting Europe in Middlefield

www.lymanorchards.com; https://specialtyproduce.com/produce/Jostaberries_15154.php; https://www.nytimes.com/2009/08/30/nyregion/30dinect.html

Ribbit!

https://www.nytimes.com/2000/12/03/nyregion/once-again-frogs-land-in-willimantic.html; *Connecticut Curiosities*; https://thechronicle.com/stories/20191018POTTERFROGS.php; http://www.ctmq.org/frog-rock

A Safari in Litchfield

https://www.actionwildlifefoundation.com/

Sergeant Stubby

https://portal.ct.gov/MIL/MAPO/History/People/Stubby-the-Military-Dog; https://amhistory.si.edu/militaryhistory/collection/object.asp?ID=15+

Shade Swamp Sanctuary
http://shadeswampct.com/shade-swamp-history/; https://www.farmington-ct.org/home/showdocument?id=3577; https://www.courant.com/news/connecticut/hc-xpm-2009-07-05-waytogo0705-art-story.html; http://www.ctmq.org/shade-swamp-sanctuary/

Slow Down and Pay Attention
Merritt Parkway Conservancy

Something to Think About
https://library.medicine.yale.edu/cushingcenter/

Spooky Fun
https://www.preservehollywood.org/

The Stepford Legacy
https://www.lockwoodmathewsmansion.com/

A Tale of Quarantine and Star-crossed Lovers
http://tollandhistorical.org/daniel-benton-homestead/; https://www.findagrave.com/memorial/65207514/elisha-benton; https://www.courant.com/community/tolland/hc-rr-tolland-benton-homestead-ghost-stories-1107-20191031-a2j4qlol35hn3bxa7lj5cux2hq-story.html; https://en.wikipedia.org/wiki/Daniel_Benton_Homestead

There's Nothing Evil in the Dark Forest
https://www.cornwallhistoricalsociety.org/

There's Something About Amy
https://windsorhistoricalsociety.org/amy-archer-gilligan-entrepreneurism-gone-wrong-in-windsor/; https://nypost.com/2014/10/17/13-things-you-probably-didnt-know-about-arsenic-and-old-lace/

Up, Up, and Away
https://www.winvian.com/cottages/helicopter/; https://connecticuthistory.org/worlds-first-helicopter-today-in-history; https://www.newenglandaviationhistory.com/tag/j-newton-williams-and-emile-berliner-helicopter/

A Walk Through the State's Military History
https://www.whmilmuseum.org/

War with Pennsylvania and Claim to Cleveland
https://www.newenglandhistoricalsociety.com/connecticut-battles-pennsylvania-pennamite-wars/; https://connecticuthistory.org/new-connecticut-on-lake-erie-connecticuts-western-reserve/; https://connecticuthistory.org/from-the-state-historian-the-map-that-wasnt-a-map/; https://explorepahistory.com/hmarker.php?markerId=1-A-178; https://case.edu/ech/articles/w/western-reserve; https://ohiohistorycentral.org/w/Connecticut_Western_Reserve; http://www.clevelandmemory.org/ellis/chap06.html; https://www.wyohistory.org/encyclopedia/wyoming-name; https://revolutionarywar.us/year-1778/battle-wyomimg-valley-massacre/ https://luzernehistory.org/event/142nd-commemoration-of-the-battle-and-massacre-at-wyoming/

What in the World is a Gungywamp?
https://diggingintothepast.org/; https://dpnc.org/gungywamp/; http://www.ct.gov/kids/lib/kids/pdf/connecticut_project_helper.pdf; https://home1.nps.gov/CRMJournal/CRM/v18n7.pdf; https://irp-cdn.multiscreensite.com/8aa1208a/files/uploaded/indian_cave_soapstone_quarry_2018_pdf.pdf

Who Ya Gonna Call?
https://tonyspera.com/; https://www.nhregister.com/lifestyle/article/Real-Annabelle-story-shared-by-Lorraine-11382545.php#item-85307-tbla-1

Whoa, Nellie!
https://www.ctfirsthorseguard.org; https://portal.ct.gov/MIL/Organization/Governors-Guards/Overview

Wild Horses Couldn't Get Me to . . .
Lake Compounce by Lynda J. Russell Arcadia Publishing, 2008; https://www.ctmq.org/
flying-horses/; https://explorenewengland.tv/adventures/exploring-the-niantic-river-ct/;
https://www.eastlymehistoricalsociety.org/index_files/Page1095.htm#goldenspur; https://
connecticuthistory.org/lake-compounce-bringing-amusements-to-the-states-residents-
since-1846/; https://www.loc.gov/; https://www.chicagotribune.com/news/ct-xpm-1991-
08-25-9103030617-story.html; https://atlanticmirror.com/anthropology-and-history/people/
death-defying-40ft-jumps-from-above-the-high-diving-horsewomen-of-atlantic-city/20/; https://
www.berkshireeagle.com/opinion/columnists/baby-boomer-memories-the-story-behind-the-
picture-of-the-pontoosuc-diving-horse/article_efb9c7d9-4497-59e2-a699-3271505e454c.html;
https://4fcnv11m92gc2af27m2ykt5w-wpengine.netdna-ssl.com/wp-content/uploads/2019/07/
MF_July17_press_release_7.17.pdf

Willimantic Rocks
https://www.wili.com/parademusic/

Witness to History
Greenwich Historical Society YouTube channel; http://radiantrootsboricuabranches.com/
hangroot-was-our-hood-reclaiming-black-greenwich-history/; https://www.henson.com/
jimsredbook/2014/05/5241969/

A Woodstock Nakation
https://www.solairrl.com/; https://www.bostonglobe.com/lifestyle/travel/2019/08/27/the-
naked-truth-conn-nudist-resort-you-can-hide-behind-fancy-clothes-you-have-yourself-here/
AqhW8ufUIugkwb2H3Jwv2H/story.html

Would You Like a Tour of Hell?
https://connecticuthistory.org/notorious-new-gate-prison/; https://www.
eastgranbyhistoricalsociety.org/; https://todayincthistory.com/2019/12/22/december-22-
newgate-prison-receives-and-quickly-loses-its-first-inmate/; https://www.youtube.com/
channel/UCZ4yXFEXvymDV5wkIt7tAcg

You Can Go Home Again
https://www.newenglandhistoricalsociety.com/why-connecticut-sent-henry-obookiah-back-
hawaii-175-years-after-he-died; http://imagesofoldhawaii.com/wp-content/uploads/Opukahaia.
pdf; https://yipap.yale.edu/news/yale-indigenous-performing-arts-travels-cornwall-connecticut

INDEX